CLASSIC

CLASSIC Cubs

A TRIBUTE TO THE MEN AND MAGIC OF WRIGLEY FIELD

JOHN HANLEY

AND

CHRIS DE LUCA

CUMBERLAND HOUSE
NASHVILLE, TENNESSEE

CLASSIC CUBS
PUBLISHED BY CUMBERLAND HOUSE PUBLISHING INC.
431 Harding Industrial Drive
Nashville, TN 37211–3160

Cover design: Gore Studio, Inc.
Text design: John Mitchell

Library of Congress Cataloging-in-Publication Data

Hanley, John, 1962
 Classic Cubs : a tribute to the men and magic of Wrigley Field / John Hanley and Chris De Luca.
  p. cm.
 Includes index.
 ISBN-13: 978-1-58182-637-1 (hardcover : alk. paper)
 ISBN-10: 1-58182-637-0 (hardcover : alk. paper)
 1. Chicago Cubs (Baseball team)—History. 2. Baseball—Illinois—Chicago—History. 3. Chicago Cubs (Baseball team)—History—Pictorial works. 4. Baseball—Illinois—Chicago—History—Pictorial works. I. De Luca, Chris, 1963- II. Title.
 GV875.C6H36 2007
 796.357'640977311—dc22

                                                          2007046056

Printed in China

1 2 3 4 5 6 7—14 13 12 11 10 09 08

To my friend Randy Salerno.
Death is more universal than life; everyone dies, but not everyone lives.
You, my friend, lived and were loved.
Godspeed, Tuff Nuts.

— J. H.

To my wife, Jill, and our children, Charlotte, Henry, and William,
for letting me escape into this fun world,
and to John Hanley,
for including me in his wonderful project

— C. D.

CONTENTS

FOREWORD I

Baseball has been a major part of my life, but it's never been my only sporting passion. Growing up in Canada, in addition to playing baseball like many other kids, I also played hockey and basketball. Everyone played hockey.

I was signed out of my high school in Chatham, Ontario, at the age of 18 and was able to share 21 years of professional baseball, which was a dream come true for me. I am very honored to have been inducted into the National Baseball Hall of Fame in Cooperstown in 1991. It is a great honor to share that designation with some of the greatest Chicago Cubs of all time—Ernie Banks, Billy Williams, and most recently Ryne Sandberg.

John Hanley's new book, *Classic Cubs: A Tribute to the Men and Magic of Wrigley Field*, is a real tribute to his work ethic, for it took tremendous amounts of time and effort to put together these moments of Cubs history under a single cover. In my humble opinion, John's art collection is second to none, and I'm proud to be a part of this book.

— *Ferguson Jenkins*
Cubs pitcher, 1966–73, 1982–83
Hall of Fame 1991

FOREWORD II

I walked onto Wrigley Field for the first time in 1982. I was still a young, inexperienced player, but I knew at that point that I wanted to play in Chicago for the rest of my career. Whoever knew that it would last 15 seasons and end with a Hall of Fame induction in 2005?

Wrigley Field was home to me. I can't say enough about the thousands of fans who would show up every day of the summer to watch the Cubs. Where else can a baseball game sell out on a Wednesday afternoon in April? Cubs fans are the greatest fans in the world, and I am so fortunate to have played my entire career in front of them.

In 2005, I had the honor of being inducted into the Baseball Hall of Fame. It's an honor that is very special to me. I was able to sit in a room with Johnny Bench, Willie Mays, and Billy Williams and call them my peers. I grew up watching these players without ever thinking that I could be placed in the same category of their elite status.

Classic Cubs is a living tribute to everything that is special about one of the greatest baseball organizations ever. I'd like to thank John Hanley and Chris De Luca for their artistic vision and historic account of the Cubs. Go Cubs!

— Ryne Sandberg
Cubs second baseman, 1982–97
Hall of Fame 2005

ACKNOWLEDGMENTS

Every Cubs fan has a moment that calls to mind everything about what being a Cubs fan is, was, or could be. For me, that is captured sitting in Grandpa's living room listening to Jack Brickhouse's trademark call on the Philco TV, "Back, back, back . . . Hey-hey!" as a Cubs home run sailed into the left-field bleachers. Thank you, Dad and Grandpa, for passing on the love of the greatest game in the world—baseball.

I would like to thank Publisher Ron Pitkin and Editor John Mitchell at Cumberland House Publishing for sharing their enthusiasm and having faith in this concept, and everyone in marketing for their assistance.

My sincere thanks to Chris De Luca, columnist for the *Chicago Sun-Times*, for lending his writing talents (during an incredibly busy baseball season) and believing in my ideas.

Thanks also to Ed Hartig and Brian Bernardoni for their expertise on Cubs and Wrigley Field history, and to Matt Boltz at WGN Radio for opening some doors for me. I'm grateful to Fergie Jenkins, Derrek Lee, Ron Santo, Pat Hughes, Len Kasper, Bob Brenly, Lena McDonagh, and Mike Huang with the Cubs for supporting my artwork.

To my instructors at the American Academy of Art, the late Fred Berger and Vern Stake, I am thankful for your inspiration and for seeing something in me at a time when I couldn't see it.

I am deeply indebted to anyone who has bought or commissioned my paintings and prints. Your appreciation, kind words, and interest in my artwork are truly a blessing.

To Jeff O'Connor and Dave Murphy, a deep debt of gratitude for helping me at all the Cubs Conventions, and thanks for all the laughs and especially for your encouragement in moving the book forward. Thanks also to Anne O'Connor, Jeff's much better half, for her advice and guidance into the publishing world.

To all my friends and neighbors, thanks for your support, friendship, and great parties. A big shout out to the Salernos for their media savvy and memorable family vacations.

To my kids—Olivia, Joey, and Ty—the happiest moments of my life have been with you.

But most of all, to my wife, Carol, I am especially grateful to you. From art school through a dreadful apprenticeship in an art studio straight out of hell to the whole "starving artist" era, you have always been there and pointed me in directions I never would have found on my own. You are still "the coolest chick in town." I will always love you.

—John Hanley

INTRODUCTION

I have, undoubtedly, one of the best jobs in all of sports, calling play-by-play for the Chicago Cubs. I don't think there is any more you could ask than to take that seat up in the booth of beautiful Wrigley Field. To think that I am sitting in the same seat as some of the greatest announcers in the history of the game, going back to Bert Wilson, Jack Brickhouse, Lou Boudreau, Vince Lloyd, Harry Caray, and of course my broadcast partner, Ron Santo, is an honor and a privilege.

There is a certain warmth that, to me, has always been a part of this franchise, and the connection between the fans and the Cubs is unparalleled in all of baseball. This beautifully painted book by John Hanley brings that connection to the reader. It is a unique baseball treasure that is a magical journey through the tradition of 134 years of Chicago Cubs baseball.

John's artwork celebrates the glorious history and milestones in vivid, rich colors and brings back some truly great moments in baseball history. He has captured the spirit of the Cubs and the unmistakable aura of the greatest ballpark in the world, Wrigley Field.

From the great Cap Anson and the double-play combination of Tinker to Evers to Chance, to the intensity of Hack Wilson and the energy of Ernie Banks, the legendary ballplayers are all beautifully rendered in John's unique style.

Overall, it is the true love of the game that John brings to this project. This is a compelling collection that all Cubs fans, baseball fans, and art lovers everywhere will appreciate for years to come.

— *Pat Hughes*
Cubs play-by-play announcer, 1996–present

CLASSIC

GROVER CLEVELAND ALEXANDER
CAP ANSON
ERNIE BANKS
THREE-FINGER BROWN
KIKI CUYLER
GABBY HARTNETT
BILLY HERMAN
FERGUSON JENKINS
RYNE SANDBERG
BRUCE SUTTER
JOE TINKER, JOHNNY EVERS, FRANK CHANCE
BILLY WILLIAMS
HACK WILSON

CLASSIC

HALL OF FAME
PLAYERS

24

Cash-strapped Phillies owner William Baker sent three-time 30-game winner Grover Cleveland Alexander and his personal catcher, "Reindeer" Bill Killefer, to the Cubs for pitcher "Iron" Mike Prendergast, catcher Pickles Dillhoefer, and $55,000 in December 1917.

The Cubs—coming off a fifth-place finish—believed the star right-hander was their missing ingredient. But "Old Pete" made just three starts for the 1918 Cubs before being drafted into the Army. He served on the front line in France during World War I, where he suffered from shell shock that left him with a permanent hearing loss and increasingly worse seizures related to epilepsy.

Alexander's best years were with the Phillies (1911–1917) as he won 190 games—one-third of the team's total over that

GROVER CLEVELAND
ALEXANDER

span—but he still won 128 games for the Cubs. His Cubs career was doomed with the arrival of new manager Joe McCarthy, who had no tolerance for Alexander's drinking. The Cubs sent the future Hall of Famer to the rival Cardinals in 1926 for the $6,000 waiver price. Alexander put on a pitching display that fall against the Yankees to help the Cards win the 1926 World Series.

After winning 373 games during a 20-year career, Alexander was in and out of sanitariums but was able to attend his induction ceremony at Cooperstown in 1938. He died broke and alone in 1950.

OLD JUDGE CIGARETTES Goodwin & Co., New York.

Adrian Constantine "Cap" Anson was one of the innovators who helped shape major-league baseball during the 19th century, getting credit for helping create spring training, pitching rotations, signals, and the hit-and-run play.

Anson enjoyed a 27-year major-league career, batting better than .300 in 20 of those seasons. As player/manager for Chicago's National League team—then known as the White Stockings or Colts— Anson won 1,283 games and five pennants. When he was fired by team President James Hart after the 1897 season, the Colts were briefly called the Orphans to reflect the departure of the man known sometimes as "Pop," "Uncle," or "Grandpa."

CAP ANSON

The right-handed-hitting Anson excelled during the Dead-Ball Era, whether facing pitchers from 45 feet away, 55 feet or the current 60 feet, 6 inches. Despite hitting .395 in 1894, Anson came under fire from sportswriters, who thought he should end his playing days in 1895 at the age of 43. Anson responded by hitting .335 and driving in 91 runs in 1895.

Anson also was famous for being a racist and was one of the major-league's key leaders in keeping black players out of the game. Late in life, he was financially ruined and baseball tried to establish a pension fund for Anson, but he rejected the offer. He was inducted into the Hall of Fame by the veterans' committee in 1939.

ERNIE
BANKS

Mr. Cub was the original *Natural*, never playing in the minor leagues and going to a high school that didn't have a baseball team. Ernest Banks wound up as the most popular Cub of all time, thanks to his exceptional power hitting and bubbly personality made famous by his refrain, "It's a beautiful day for a ballgame. . . . Let's play two!"

Banks and Gene Baker became the first black players to wear a Cubs uniform, joining the team in 1953. Banks, who had starred for the Negro Leagues' Kansas City Monarchs, helped redefine the role of shortstop in the major leagues, blending power, a high average, and Gold Glove defense.

He won back-to-back MVP Awards in 1958 and '59. From 1955 to 1960, no one—including contemporaries Henry Aaron, Willie Mays, or Mickey Mantle—hit more homers than Banks. Injuries late in his career reduced Banks's range at short, and he moved to first base.

On May 25, 1962, Cincinnati Reds pitcher Moe Drabowsky beaned Banks, who was taken off the field on a stretcher. Four days later, Banks returned to the lineup and hit three home runs and a double against the Milwaukee Braves at Wrigley Field.

Banks became the first Cubs player to have his uniform number retired when No. 14 was honored on August 22, 1982—five years after his election to the Hall of Fame.

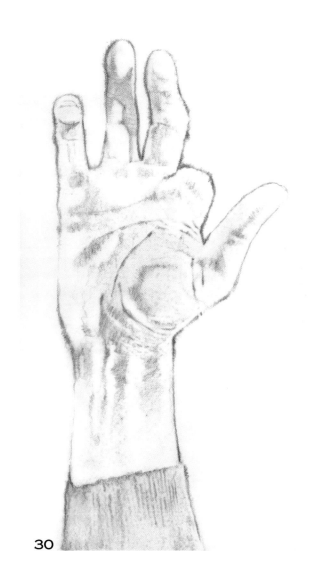

As a 7-year-old playing on his uncle's farm in Indiana, Mordecai Peter Centennial Brown mangled his right hand in a corn grinder. The accident cost him his forefinger and disfigured his middle and pinkie fingers. A terrible accident, but Brown was left with a pitching hand that could spin off one of the greatest curveballs of all time.

Nicknamed "Three-Finger" by sportswriters, Brown was simply called "Miner" by his teammates, who knew the converted infielder had toiled in the coal mines before starting a baseball career at the age of 24.

With the double-play combination of Tinker to Evers to Chance playing behind him, Brown was the ace pitcher on the Cubs' powerhouse teams that won consecutive World Series in 1907 and '08. He had six straight 20-win seasons and relished his duels with fellow National League ace Christy Mathewson, once winning nine consecutive matchups against his rival.

Famous for his top fitness and durability, Brown often worked out of the bullpen between starts, leading the NL four times in saves. He totaled 48 saves during his career.

A 239-game winner—with a .648 winning percentage—during a 14-year career, Brown was inducted into the Hall of Fame in 1949.

THREE-FINGER
BROWN

KIKI
CUYLER

Hazen Shirley "Kiki" Cuyler could run, hit, and field, all with grace. Plus, he could wow fans with his all-American image that was honed during his West Point days before World War I.

Cuyler came to the Cubs in 1928 after a solid career with the Pirates, joining Hack Wilson and Riggs Stephenson to form one of the greatest outfields of all time. He helped the Cubs win the pennant in 1929, using his speed on the bases after rifling line drives to all fields.

During his career, he hit .300 or better 10 times and topped .350 four times. While playing for the Pirates in 1925, Cuyler hit safely in 10 consecutive at-bats, setting a National League record that still stands.

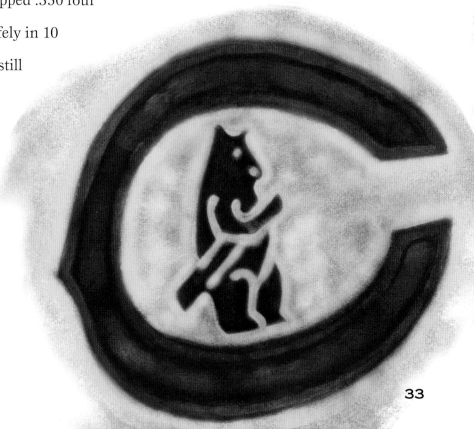

His nickname has some odd roots. His minor-league teammates called him "Cuy"—rhymes with eye—for short. When the shortstop and second baseman would yell out his name on short flies to the outfield, fans would hear "Cuy, Cuy." Writers in the press box turned this into "Kiki," and a nickname was born.

The veterans' committee voted Cuyler—considered a marginal candidate—into the Hall of Fame in 1968.

34

GABBY
HARTNETT

When Charles Leo Hartnett joined the Cubs in 1922, his incessant chatter and jovial attitude—leading to his nickname "Gabby"—were backed up by his enormous talent.

Considered the best catcher in the National League during the first half of the 20th century, Hartnett will always be remembered by Cubs fans for his "Homer in the Gloamin'"—a dramatic tiebreaking home run by the player/manager against the Pirates at Wrigley Field in 1938 that helped put the Cubs in first place and on the way toward a pennant.

The oldest of 14 children, Hartnett seemed to have been born into the job. His father was semipro catcher with a strong arm. Gabby had a strong arm and swung a deadly bat.

Though sidetracked by injuries early in his career, Hartnett caught 100 or more games 12 times for the Cubs. He was behind the plate in the 1934 All-Star Game when Carl Hubbell set a record by striking out Babe Ruth, Lou Gehrig, Jimmie Foxx, Al Simmons, and Joe Cronin in succession.

As a manager, Hartnett compiled a 203–176 record but was fired by the Cubs after a fifth-place finish in 1940. He spent the next year with the Giants, hitting .300 as a 40-year-old catcher/pinch hitter before retiring.

Hartnett, who was inducted into the Hall of Fame in 1955, died of cirrhosis in Park Ridge, Illinois, on his 72nd birthday.

When it was time for the Cubs to replace future Hall of Famer Rogers Hornsby at second base, they turned to William Jennings Bryan Herman in 1932.

Billy Herman went on to become the best second baseman of the 1930s, providing dazzling defense and sharpshooting offense. He was considered one of the best hit-and-run men of his era and hit .304 during his career, batting mostly in the No. 2 spot.

Herman rarely struck out and was considered one of baseball's craftiest players because of his knack for stealing signs and decking unsuspecting base runners.

From 1932 through 1938, Herman teamed with shortstop Billy Jurges to form a stingy double-play combination that helped the Cubs win three National League pennants. His best offensive season came in 1935, when he played in every game, hitting .341 with a league-high 227 hits, helping the Cubs win the pennant.

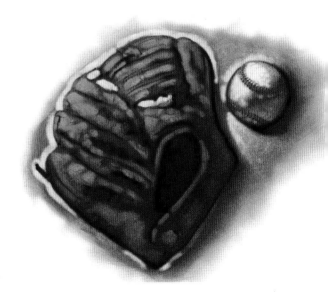

While playing for the Brooklyn Dodgers in 1943, Herman hit .330 with a .398 on-base percentage and 100 RBI. He missed the next two seasons while serving in World War II but returned to the Dodgers in 1946.

Herman was inducted into the Hall of Fame in 1975.

38

When manager Leo Durocher acquired 6–5, 210-pound right-hander Ferguson Arthur Jenkins from the Phillies early in the 1966 season, he took the big reliever and immediately put him in the rotation. Jenkins validated the move by winning at least 20 games each season from 1967 through 1972.

In 1971, Jenkins became the first Canadian and first Cubs pitcher to win the National League Cy Young Award, going 24–13 with a 2.77 ERA. But what stands out most might be Jenkins's durability that season. He made 39 starts and pitched 30 complete games—walking just 37 batters in 325 innings. He also hit six home runs and knocked in 20 runs in 115 at-bats.

After Jenkins's 20-win streak ended in 1973, the Cubs needed a third baseman to replace the aging Ron Santo, so Jenkins was dealt to the Rangers for Bill Madlock. In his first start for the Rangers, Jenkins pitched a one-hitter, shutting out the A's in the middle of their World Series dynasty run.

Jenkins went from the Rangers to the Red Sox before returning to the Cubs as a free agent in 1982. At the age of 38, he led the Cubs in innings ($217^{1}/_{3}$) and ERA (3.15) while compiling a 14–15 record.

The Cubs' all-time strikeout leader was inducted into the Hall of Fame in 1991.

FERGIE
JENKINS

RYNE
SANDBERG

After general manager Dallas Green acquired Ryne Sandberg from the Phillies before the 1982 season, the Cubs weren't sure what to do with the talented young player, trying him in center field and at third base before moving to his permanent home at second base.

Sandberg started his Cubs career with a 1-for-31 slump before becoming one of the most dangerous hitters ever to play second base—appearing in 10 consecutive All-Star Games. But he was more than just an offensive weapon, winning nine consecutive Gold Gloves, playing 123 straight games without an error, and going four seasons without a throwing error.

His Hall of Fame credentials were sealed during a nationally televised game at Wrigley Field against the Cardinals on June 23, 1984. "Ryno" went 5-for-6 with seven RBI and belted tying home runs in the ninth and 10th innings off future Hall of Famer Bruce Sutter, overshadowing the performance of Cardinals outfielder Willie McGee, who hit for the cycle and had already been tabbed NBC's player of the game before Sandberg's first homer. The Cubs won 12–11 in 11 innings.

During a surprisingly stirring induction speech at Cooperstown in 2005, the normally soft-spoken Sandberg chided today's selfish players and stressed the importance of respecting the game.

Sandberg's number 23 was retired by the Cubs on August 28, 2005.

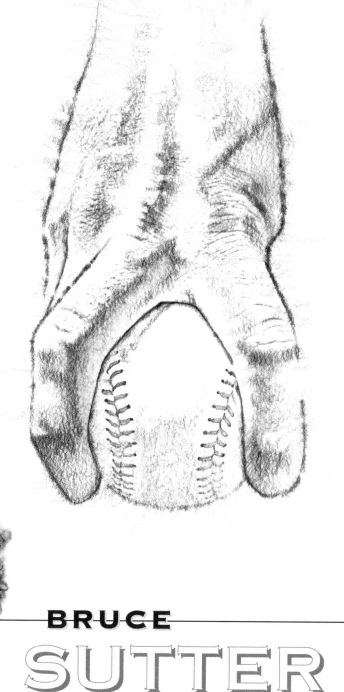

After undergoing elbow surgery in 1972—an operation he tried to keep a secret from the Cubs—Howard Bruce Sutter lost his fastball and figured his career was over. The following spring training, Cubs roving minor-league pitching coach Fred Martin suggested Sutter learn how to master a gimmick pitch known as the split-finger fastball.

When done right, the split-finger mimics a fastball, then falls off the table before reaching the plate. The hitter usually is left to look silly. Armed with this new pitch, Sutter helped define the role of closer and brought respect to relievers.

During the 1979 season, when he won the National League Cy Young Award, Sutter won six games and earned 37 saves, giving him a key role in more than half of the Cubs' 80 victories.

After the '79 season, Sutter won a salary-arbitration battle with the Cubs and was awarded a $700,000 contract for 1980—a rich deal for a reliever in those days. The right-hander earned another league-high 28 saves that year. But with Lee Smith emerging as the Cubs' next great reliever, the high-priced Sutter was dealt to the Cardinals.

When he was inducted in 2006, Sutter became the first pitcher in the Hall of Fame who never started a game.

BRUCE
SUTTER

CLASSIC CUBS

JOE JOHNNY FRANK

TINKER EVERS CHANCE

Tinker to Evers to Chance—the Cubs' double-play combination from their 1908 World Series-winning team struck fear in National League opponents and inspired *New York Evening Mail* columnist Franklin Pierce Adams to immortalize the trio with his poem titled "Baseball's Sad Lexicon" in 1910.

The elite double-play combination—with Joe Tinker at short, Johnny Evers at second, and Frank Chance at first—never led the league in turning two. Historians have debated that Adams's poem did more to get the three into the Hall of Fame—via the Veterans' Committee in 1946—than their actual play.

The sad reality is that Tinker and Evers hated each other—they once had a fistfight on the field over a cab-fare dispute—but were the heart of a team that won four pennants in five seasons with Chance as player/manager. Chance was 27 when he took over managing duties and compiled a 768–389 record as Cubs manager. His .664 winning percentage remains the best in club history.

The Tinker-Evers feud lasted for decades, with the two former teammates refusing to speak to each other. But when the Cubs played in the 1938 World Series, both were invited back to take part in the radio broadcast. When they came face to face—after a nervous silence—the two embraced, bringing each other to tears.

BASEBALL'S SAD LEXICON

By Franklin P. Adams

These are the saddest of possible words

Tinker to Evers to Chance.

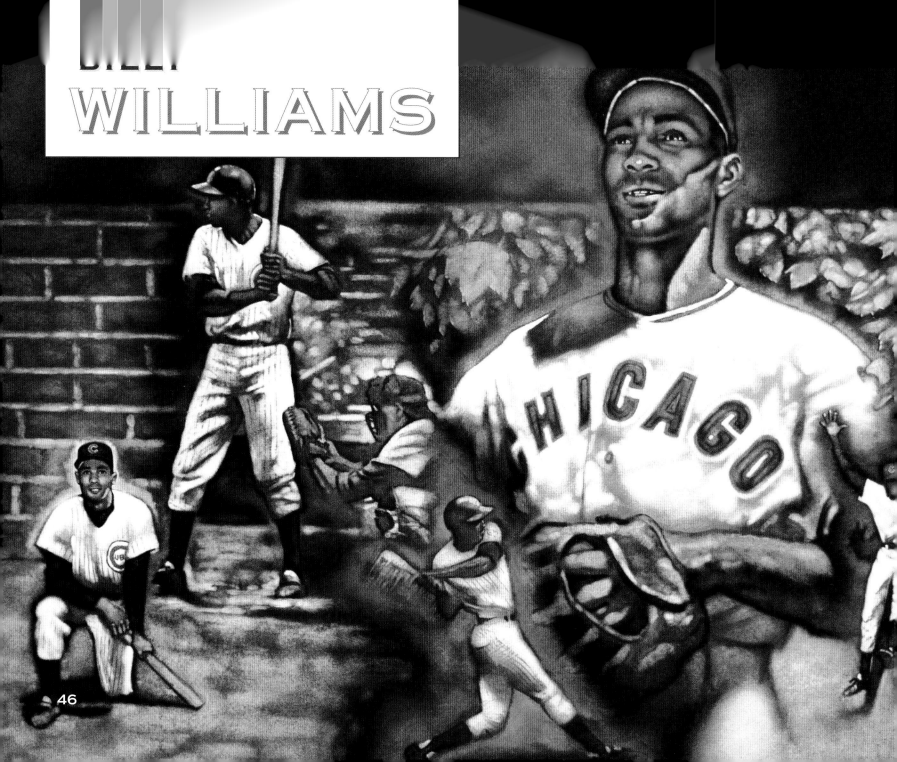

BILLY
WILLIAMS

The sweet swing of left-handed-hitting outfielder Billy Leo Williams was the perfect blend of power and grace. Nicknamed "Whistler" after his hometown in Alabama, Williams was a quiet leader who built his reputation on consistency and durability.

He quietly became a mainstay on Cubs teams that had more popular players in Ernie Banks and Ron Santo. But from September 22, 1963, to September 2, 1970, Williams played in 1,117 consecutive games, setting a National League record that was broken in 1983 by Steve Garvey.

The Cubs never finished higher than second place with Williams, but he consistently delivered winning numbers, hitting 20 or more home runs in 14 seasons and driving in at least 90 runs in 10 seasons. On September 10, 1968, against the Mets, he hit three home runs in one game for the first time in his career. It came a game after he hit two runs, tying a major-league record with five home runs in two games.

Hall of Famer Rogers Hornsby, a roving instructor for the team, pushed the Cubs to promote Williams to the majors after working with him in the Texas League.

Williams joined Hornsby in the Hall of Fame in 1987 and had his jersey number 26 retired that same year by the Cubs.

47

HACK
WILSON

Acquired from the New York Giants in a heavily disputed postseason draft, the Cubs paid just $5,000 for new cleanup hitter Lewis Robert "Hack" Wilson before the 1926 season. Wilson was not the prototypical center fielder. He stood 5 feet 6, weighed at least 195 pounds, boasted an 18-inch neck, but needed size-6 shoes. Playing for the Cubs in 1930, he turned in a phenomenal season—even by the standards of today's post-steroid era.

Wilson hit .356 and drew a league-leading 105 walks. But his best work came in the power department. Wilson belted 56 home runs—a National League record that stood until 1998. His 191 RBI—breaking his record of 159 set the season before—remains a record today, and many believe it will stay unmatched. He reached that total without a single grand slam. Keep in mind, when Barry Bonds hit 73 home runs, he had just 137 RBI.

Lewis Robert Wilson got his nickname, "Hack," either from old-time wrestler George Hackenschmidt or from an earlier Cub and fan favorite, Hack Miller, who also was built like a fireplug. Despite a flair for showmanship, Wilson's career was derailed by alcoholism—he had multiple arrests in Chicago for violating Prohibition—leading to his premature death.

Wilson died alone and penniless at 48. His body was left unclaimed by family at the morgue. His election to the Hall of Fame in 1979 had been delayed for years on "moral grounds."

49

WEST SIDE GROUNDS

WEEGHMAN PARK

WRIGLEY FIELD

2

CLASSIC *Cubs*

THE BALLPARKS

WEST SIDE
GROUNDS

West Side Grounds was home to the Cubs during their golden era, when the double-play combination of Tinker to Evers to Chance was striking fear in opponents and Three-Finger Brown was baffling hitters on the mound.

In May 1893, the Cubs—then known as the Colts—moved into Chicago's first double-decked stadium, West Side Grounds, located on a patch of land bordered by Taylor, Wood, Polk, and Lincoln (now Wolcott) streets. This would be the Cubs' home for the next 23 years.

Originally, only Sunday games were played at West Side Grounds, with the remaining home games played in 1893 at South Side Park—near what would become Comiskey Park and home to the White Sox. By 1894, the Cubs played all of their home games at West Side Grounds. The first modern World Series was played there in 1906—between the Cubs and White Sox. It is the site of the Cubs' last World Series championship, in 1908. But the most dramatic—and frightful— event occurred during its first season, when a cigar thrown in the trash sparked a fire at the wooden ballpark.

Panicked fans pressed against the barbed-wire fences trying to escape as the fire spread through the first-base stands. Several players—including Walt Wilmot and Jimmy Ryan wielding bats—jumped into the seats and broke through the fence to create an escape route for fans. The day after the fire, baseball went on, with the scorched area roped off.

By 1915, West Side Grounds was showing its age, thanks in large part to penny-pinching owner Charles Murphy's neglect, and the Cubs were ready for a move to the North Side.

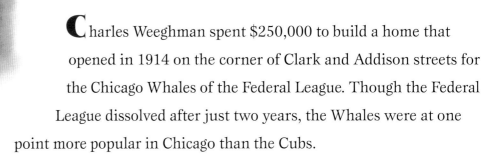

Charles Weeghman spent $250,000 to build a home that opened in 1914 on the corner of Clark and Addison streets for the Chicago Whales of the Federal League. Though the Federal League dissolved after just two years, the Whales were at one point more popular in Chicago than the Cubs.

Weeghman and a group of investors that included William Wrigley Jr. bought the Cubs and moved them into Weeghman Park on April 20, 1916. The Cubs beat the Cincinnati Reds 7–6 in 11 innings that day, and a bear cub was in attendance.

The original structure was a single-deck stadium designed by architect Zachary Taylor Davis, who also helped build Comiskey Park for the White Sox. Before a ballpark was built, the land had been occupied by the Chicago Lutheran Theological Seminary, adding to the "Hallowed Grounds" legend.

From 1920 through '25, the stadium was called Cubs Park. After some expansion in 1926, the ballpark was renamed Wrigley Field. The famous ivy covering the outfield walls didn't appear until 1937.

WEEGHMAN PARK

BLEACHERS
EST. PRICE 50¢
TAX PAID 5¢
TOTAL 55¢

WRIGLEY FIELD
HOME OF
CHICAGO CUBS

SPALDING
Official
National League

WRIGLEY
FIELD

Wrigley Field is the crown jewel of ballparks. From its ivy-covered walls to its manually operated scoreboard to its bright green expanse of natural grass, Wrigley boasts the kind of charm many of the new "retro" ballparks try so hard to copy. The second-oldest ballpark in the majors—younger than only Fenway Park in Boston—is nestled in a beautiful North Side neighborhood known as Wrigleyville. A trip to Wrigley Field is pure nostalgia, with corner taverns, red-brick Fire Engine House No. 78 (built in 1915) behind the left-field wall, and the rumble of the Red Line el trains beyond the right-center bleachers.

WRIGLEY FIELD
HOME OF
CHICAGO CUBS

58

NATIONAL

UMPIRES

BATTER
2

SAMMY SOSA
.295 51 HR 112 RBI

CHICAGO
CUBS

BLEACHER GATE N

FRIENDLY CONFINES

Ernie Banks, "Mr. Cub," helped popularize one of Wrigley Field's famous nicknames—"The Friendly Confines." Among the many landmarks is the red-and-white marquee looming over the corner of Clark and Addison that reads, "Wrigley Field Home of Chicago Cubs."

The old-time 27- by-75-foot green scoreboard—sitting 85 feet about the field—was built in 1937 at the urging of Bill Veeck. The 10-foot-diameter clock was added in 1941. The flags flapping over Sheffield Avenue indicate the direction of the unpredictable winds blowing toward or away from Lake Michigan.

William Wrigley Jr. took over controlling ownership of the Cubs after Charles Weeghman's debts mounted and he was forced to sell. One of Wrigley's first moves was hiring William Veeck as team president.

In the following years, Cubs Park underwent massive changes. Wrigley and Veeck brought in original architect Zachary Taylor Davis to consult on renovations from 1922 through '28. A second deck was added above the grandstands, boosting capacity to 38,396. Temporary bleachers were added in 1929, '32, and '35 to accommodate larger crowds during winning seasons. The Cubs even allowed overflow crowds to watch games from behind ropes in the outfield and to walk the field after games.

In 1937, Wrigley Field began to take on its present configuration under the direction of a young Bill Veeck, who had been hired after the death of his father, William. As a 23-year-old former office boy, Bill Veeck was trusted with a drastic makeover of the ballpark. New bleachers were built, providing a home to a whole new culture of Cubs fans. The ballpark's dimensions changed to the current 355 feet to left field, 400 feet to near-straightaway center, and 353 feet to right.

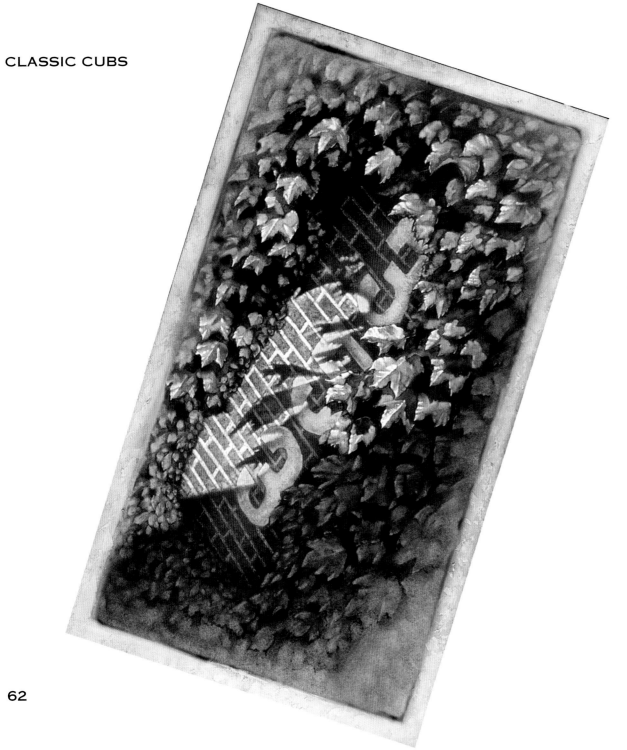

Veeck also ordered Chinese elm trees and potted plants for the bleacher areas. He planted Boston ivy and Japanese bittersweet plants on the outfield walls, giving Wrigley Field its unique look. The fierce winds blowing off Lake Michigan destroyed the trees and potted plants, but the ivy survived. House rules provide that any ball stuck in the ivy is a ground-rule double.

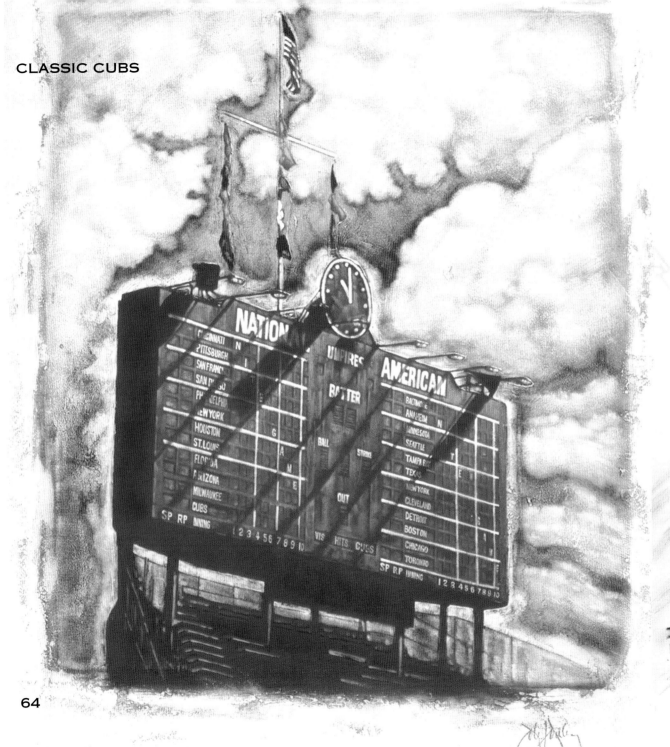

Though no match for today's DiamondVision screens, Wrigley Field's old-fashioned scoreboard is beloved by fans. The massive structure was based on a local inventor's plans which featured magnetic "eyelids" that closed manually for the numbers that tracked balls and strikes. Inside the scoreboard, panels are turned manually by workers balancing on ladders to post scores and innings.

BLEACHER BUMS

They called themselves "Bums," but to Cubs fans, they were bigger than life. In 1966, a group of 10 fans who met at a tavern on the corner of Waveland and Sheffield called Ray's Bleachers took their act to the left-field cheap seats and formed a legendary piece of Cubs history. The "Bleacher Bums" grew in popularity when a fan stuck his head through a bull's eye on a sign that read, "HIT THE BLEACHER BUM."

The "Bums" rallied around manager Leo Durocher and towel-waving pitcher Dick Selma. Cubs fever soared from there, and the "Bums" even took their act on the road.

The "Bleacher Bums" have been immortalized in stage plays and in music but are now just a memory—replaced by high ticket prices and cell-phone-toting posers looking for a frat party at what has become known as "Chicago's biggest beer garden."

TURN ON THE
LIGHTS

Wrigley Field might have been the first ballpark to have lights, but they weren't used for baseball. Owner Charles Weeghman had a complete electrical lighting system installed, but those lights were used only to illuminate postgame shows that featured circus acts and Vaudeville entertainers.

P. K. Wrigley purchased lights for his stadium in 1941, and they were transported to Wrigley Field for installation. But with the outbreak of World War II, the steel was donated instead to the war effort.

In the early 1980s, as postseason baseball moved to night games to accommodate wider television audiences, Wrigley Field—the only holdout—was faced with a threat from Major League Baseball: install lights or move any postseason games to Comiskey Park or Busch Stadium in St. Louis.

On February 25, 1988, the Chicago City Council repealed a 1983 ordinance banning night games at Wrigley Field. MLB rewarded the city by awarding the 1990 All-Star Game to Wrigley Field, which also hosted the Midsummer Classic in 1947 and 1962.

The six 33-foot-high light towers that blended so well with Wrigley's architecture were turned on in August 1988. The originally scheduled "first" night game was rained out in the fourth inning on August 8 but took place the next night, when the Cubs beat the New York Mets 6–4.

THE BEARS AT
CUBS PARK

Wrigley Field might be known as one of the most treasured baseball parks in the major leagues, but it has hosted more professional football games than any other venue. Owner George Halas brought his Decatur Staleys pro football team to Chicago in 1921, and Wrigley Field was their home until 1970. With his team starting out at a place called Cubs Park, Halas renamed the Staleys the Bears in 1922 to identify more with the baseball team—a common practice in those days.

Converting a baseball diamond into a gridiron was fairly simple at most stadiums, but Wrigley's unique dimensions required a little creativity. The football field was laid over the infield and into left field. Bleachers were moved into right field to allow for more seating—up to 46,000 for football. Remodeling the baseball field to add more bleachers in the 1930s made an even tighter fit for football. The corner of the south end zone was actually in the visiting baseball dugout, which was outfitted with padding to protect football players. Special ground rules allowed trimming the corner of that end zone, and the corner of the north end zone was just nine yards long instead of 10 because it stopped directly at the base of the left-field brick wall.

The final years of the Bears' era at Wrigley Field were highlighted by the peak seasons for Hall of Fame running back Gale Sayers, who was the 1965 Rookie of the Year. The 332 football games played at Wrigley Field by the Bears are the most by one home team in National Football League history. But with the growth of the NFL and a need for more seating, the Bears moved out of Wrigley Field after the 1970 season. The Bears' move to Soldier Field was necessary because of an NFL rule that required a minimum seating capacity of 50,000.

The last football game played at Wrigley Field was on December 13, 1970, between the Bears and the rival Green Bay Packers. The Bears won 35–17. The Bears' record at Wrigley Field was an impressive 221–89–22.

BILL BUCKNER, BILL MADLOCK, RICK REUSCHEL
PHIL CAVARETTA
ANDRE DAWSON
MARK GRACE
CHARLIE GRIMM
STAN HACK
DAVE KINGMAN
DERREK LEE
GREG MADDUX
ARAMIS RAMIREZ
RON SANTO
HANK SAUER
ALFONSO SORIANO
SAMMY SOSA
HIPPO VAUGHN
BILLY WILLIAMS, RON SANTO, ERNIE BANKS
CARLOS ZAMBRANO

3

CLASSIC

OUTSTANDING
PLAYERS

New England will forever remember—and never forgive—Bill Buckner for letting a grounder from the New York Mets' Mookie Wilson snake between his legs during Game 6 of the 1986 World Series. But Cubs fans remember Buckner for the work he did in Chicago long before he joined the Boston Red Sox.

A solid outfielder with the Los Angeles Dodgers, Buckner was traded to the Cubs, along with shortstop Ivan DeJesus, for Rick Monday in January 1977. The Cubs converted "Billy Buck" into a first baseman—helping to ease the pressure on his chronically ailing ankles—and his career took off.

Buckner, who finished with 2,715 hits and just 453 strikeouts in 2,517 games, hit .300 during his stay with the Cubs (1977–84), won the 1980 National League batting title with a career-high .324 mark, and twice led the league in doubles (1981 and 1983).

As for that pivotal error in the 1986 World Series, there was a Cubs connection. Photos later revealed that Buckner was wearing a Cubs batting glove underneath his first baseman's mitt. The Cubs curse lived on.

Bill Madlock played for six teams during his 15 years in the major leagues, but his two seasons with the Cubs—1975–76—were among his finest. Madlock won four batting titles during his career, including two as a Cub.

Madlock, who grew up in Decatur, Illinois, has been overlooked by Hall of Fame voters primarily because his defense was mediocre and he was overshadowed during his era by Philadelphia Phillies third baseman Mike Schmidt.

Madlock's best season was in 1976, when he committed 14 errors in 136 games at third base. He won his second straight batting title that season on the final day, getting four hits against the Atlanta Braves to raise his average by six points to .339. He was in a race with the Cincinnati Reds' Ken Griffey Sr., who went 0-for-2 in the final game, dropping his average to .336.

One of the highlights of his career came on July 26, 1975, when Madlock got six hits against the New York Mets at Wrigley Field. But the Cubs lost 9–8, stranding Madlock on second base after a 10th-inning single.

A big farm boy from Quincy, Illinois, Rickey Eugene Reuschel was drafted by the Cubs from Western Illinois University in 1970. Two years later, "Big Daddy"— listed at 6 feet 4 and 225 pounds—was in their rotation.

He went 214–191 (a .528 winning percentage) during a 19-year career that included stops with the New York Yankees, Pittsburgh Pirates, and San Francisco Giants. But during two tours with the Cubs, Reuschel won 135 games.

His best season was 1977, when he was on a Cy Young pace, but faded at the end and went 20–10—the only Cubs pitcher to sandwich a 20-win season around Fergie Jenkins's 24 victories in 1971 and Greg Maddux's 20 victories in 1992.

After being traded to the Yankees in June 1981, Reuschel returned to the Cubs in 1983 and went 5–5 during their division-winning season of 1984. But in a controversial move, he was left off their postseason roster in favor of Dick Ruthven, who didn't make an appearance during the National League Championship Series against the San Diego Padres.

BILL   **BILL**   **RICK**

BUCKNER MADLOCK REUSCHEL

PHIL

CAVARETTA

When he was a left-handed pitcher attending Lane Tech High School on Chicago's North Side—hoping to become an auto mechanic—Phil Cavaretta used to slip away from school and sneak into Wrigley Field to watch the Cubs play. He soon would have a daily invitation to the ballpark.

Cavaretta, a steady-hitting first baseman, spent 20 seasons with the Cubs, from 1934 through '53, one of the longest tenures in team history. His professional baseball career started with Class A Peoria of the old Central League, and he signed his contract while still in high school. In his first game with Peoria in 1934, Cavaretta hit for the cycle. The Cubs promoted him that September, and by the next season, he was the starting first baseman for a pennant-winning team—as an 18-year-old.

Because of his hometown connection, Cavaretta became an instant star in Chicago, and he didn't disappoint. During the Cubs' World Series run in 1945, Cavaretta was named the National League MVP, and he hit .423 with seven runs and five RBI during a losing effort to the Detroit Tigers in the World Series.

Cavaretta became the Cubs' player/manager in 1951, compiling a 169–213 record before being fired in 1953. He spent the final two seasons of his career with the White Sox.

ANDRE DAWSON

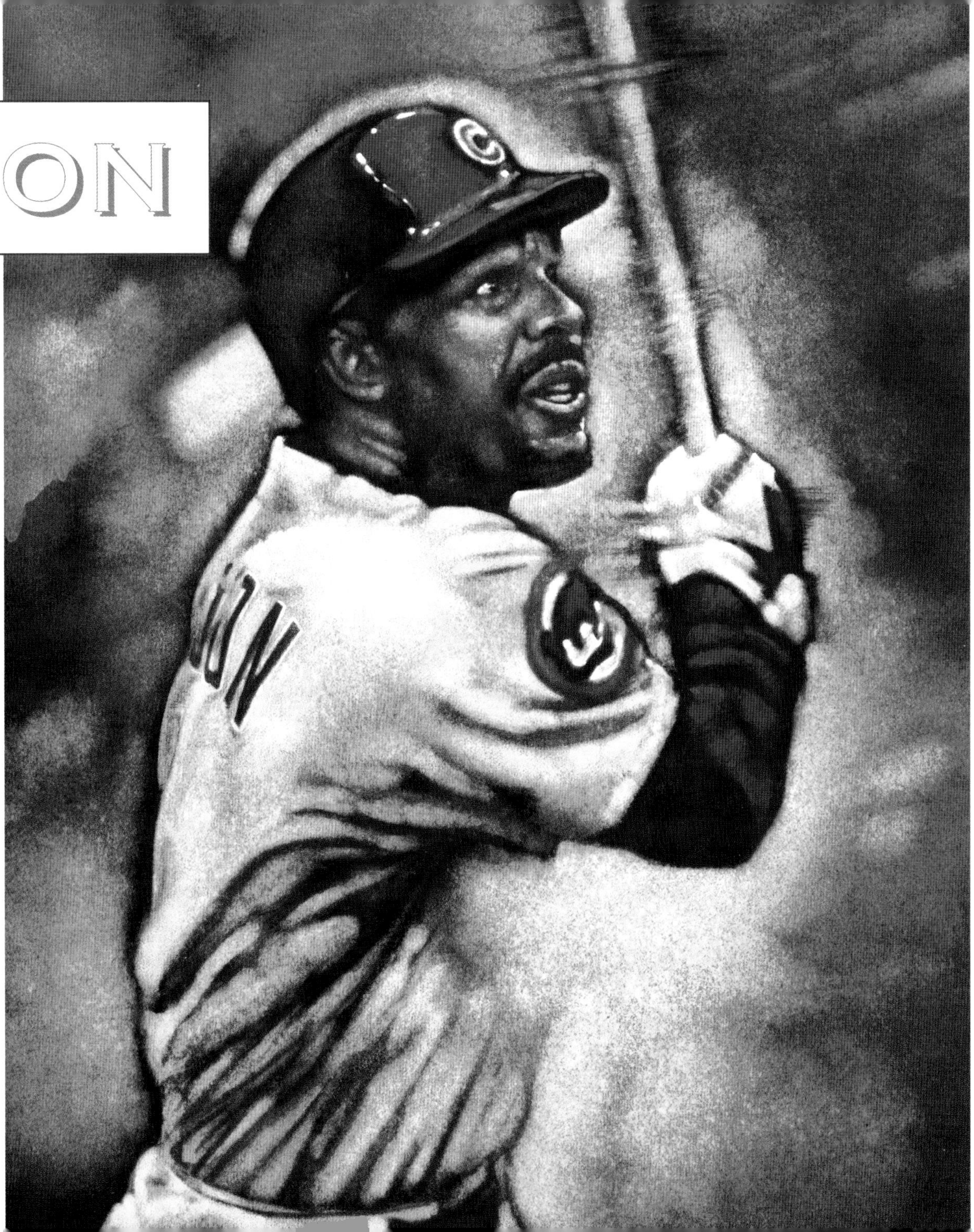

It has almost become part of the induction-ceremony tradition. In recent years—beginning with Ryne Sandberg's enshrinement in 2005—the Hall of Fame's newest members have been making pleas to get Cubs great Andre Dawson a few more votes.

"The Hawk" was drafted by the Montreal Expos in 1975 and was the National League Rookie of the Year in 1977. He spent more than 10 years with the Expos—in 1981, '82 and '83—but his most famous work was accomplished with the Cubs.

After rejecting a two-year, $2 million offer to stay in Montreal, Dawson entered into negotiations with the Cubs that eventually turned ugly. The two sides finally agreed on a one-year, $500,000 contract that allowed for an extra $150,000 if Dawson's knees held out. When the Cubs signed Dawson as a free agent in March 1987, pitching ace Rick Sutcliffe said it felt "like Christmas Eve."

And Dawson looked like a kid again playing on Wrigley Field's natural grass, belting 49 home runs and driving in a career-high 137 runs to win the National League MVP Award in 1987. He was so feared as a hitter, he drew a record five intentional walks in a 16-inning game during the 1990 season.

The Dawson signing was a steal—and he stayed with the Cubs through the 1992 season.

MARK GRACE

His power could never match that of teammates Ryne Sandberg, Andre Dawson, or Sammy Sosa, but Mark Grace became a favorite of Cubs fans for his steady work at first base and his consistent hitting at the plate.

For 13 seasons, Grace delighted Cubs fans, earning four Gold Gloves at first base and making three trips to the All-Star Game. He never hit more than 17 home runs in a season but led the league with 51 doubles in 1995. He helped lead the Cubs to the 1989 National League Championship Series and hit .647 (11-for-17) with a home run, three doubles, and eight RBI in five games against the San Francisco Giants.

Grace was so steady at the plate, he totaled more hits than anyone in the 1990s—1,754 for the decade, more than Hall of Famer Tony Gwynn's 1,713.

While Cubs fans loved "Gracie," he had a falling out with management after the 2000 season and signed as a free agent with the Arizona Diamondbacks. As with most Cubs, it took leaving town to find a World Series championship, and Grace's came his first season with the Diamondbacks. His leadoff single off New York Yankees closer Mariano Rivera in the ninth-inning of Game 7 set the stage for the Diamondbacks' classic comeback.

Charlie Grimm had his own ideas about playing first base. He preferred a small mitt and he loved to stray as far as possible off the bag. His formula was a successful one considering Grimm won nine fielding titles and was considered one of the best first basemen of his era (1916–36).

He started his career with the Pittsburgh Pirates but was traded to the Cubs—along with Wilbur Cooper and Rabbit Maranville—for Vic Aldridge, George Grantham, and Al Niehaus in October 1924. "Jolly Cholly" was known for his wit on the field and in the clubhouse.

He played in the 1929 and '32 World Series for the Cubs and hit a combined .364 (12-for-33) with a home run and five RBI in nine games. His friendly approach made him a natural as player/manager when Cubs players soured on the stern style of Rogers Hornsby. Grimm took over as manager in 1932 and led the Cubs to pennants that season, in '38, and in '45.

JOLLY CHOLLY
GRIMM

Stan Hack's smile was so famous, Cubs executive Bill Veeck Jr. put it on the back of small mirrors and sold them at Wrigley Field in 1935. The slogan was "Smile With Stan Hack," and fans loved the promotion. It soon came to an end when fans began shining the mirrors into opposing batters' eyes.

Hack did his own kind of damage to opponents. A slick-fielding third baseman, he spent his entire 16-year career (1932–47) with the Cubs, hitting .301. Never a power hitter, Hack scored at least 100 runs in seven seasons—including a stretch of six consecutive 100-run seasons from 1936 through '41.

A strained relationship with Cubs manager Jimmy Wilson led Hack to retire in 1943, but he was lured back to the team by new manager Charlie Grimm and hit a career-high .323 in 1945, helping lead the Cubs to their last World Series of the 20th century.

Hack's smile was almost as famous as his swing, and a fellow player once said Hack "has more friends than Leo Durocher has enemies."

STAN
HACK

Dave Kingman didn't just hit home runs, he hit *monster* home runs. One of the longest blasts ever to leave Wrigley Field came off the bat of Kingman on April 14, 1976, when he was playing for the New York Mets. There was a runner on first, and Cubs right-handed reliever Tom Dettore was on the mound. Kingman launched a rocket that cleared Waveland Avenue beyond the left-field bleachers and bounced in front of the fourth house on the east side of Kenmore Avenue, the street that intersects Waveland behind Wrigley Field.

For years, a red "X" marked the spot on the sidewalk of a home run that has been estimated to have traveled 550 to 600 feet in the air.

Two years later, after signing a free-agent contract with the Cubs, Kingman could call Wrigley Field home. His first May as a Cub, Kingman put on a three-homer show one game against the Los Angeles Dodgers at Wrigley Field, prompting a famous tirade from Dodgers manager Tommy Lasorda, who was asked his thoughts about Kingman's performance.

His second season with the Cubs, 1979, was the best of Kingman's career. He hit 48 home runs—the most by a Cub since Ernie Banks belted 47 homers 21 years earlier—and knocked in 115 runs. Briefly, Kingman was one of the Cubs' most popular players, but he quickly dispelled that with his eccentricities. He sent a dead rat to a female sportswriter and failed to show up for a game at which fans received a t-shirt in his honor.

DAVE

KINGMAN

First baseman Derrek Lee helped break the hearts of Cubs fans with his big hits in the 2003 National League Championship Series while playing for the Florida Marlins. The next season, he became a Cub after being acquired for young first baseman Hee Seop Choi.

At first, fans weren't sold on Lee. When he got off to a slow start in 2004—and Choi got off to a sizzling start with the Marlins—fans at Wrigley Field began chanting "Hee Seop Choi, Hee Seop Choi."

Lee soon became a fan-favorite at Wrigley, hitting .278 with 32 home runs and 98 RBI his first season in Chicago. By 2005—the Cubs' first season without slugger Sammy Sosa—Lee was on his way to establishing himself as one of baseball's premier players.

He earned his first trip the All-Star Game in 2005 by hitting a major-league-best .376, with 27 home runs and 72 RBI in the first half. He made a run at the triple crown, earning his first batting title with a .335 batting average, finishing second with 46 home runs and finishing seventh with 107 RBI.

As for the chants of "Hee Seop Choi, Hee Seop Choi," they vanished in 2004.

DERREK
LEE

GREG
MADDUX

When Greg Maddux made his Cubs debut on September 1, 1986, he looked more like one of the batboys than the team's future ace, standing 6 feet tall and weighing 150 pounds.

Maddux had just gone 10–1 in 18 starts for Class AAA Iowa when he was part of the Cubs' expanded roster that September. Dressing in the Cubs' tiny Wrigley Field clubhouse, Maddux's locker was next to ace Rick Sutcliffe's. Maddux pulled on his uniform and quietly said to Sutcliffe, "I guess I should get out there for batting practice?"

"With the kind of year you've had," Sutcliffe replied, "you can do anything you want."

That meant stringing together a Hall of Fame-caliber career.

Maddux became the first pitcher to win four consecutive Cy Young Awards (1992–1995). His first came in '92 with the Cubs. After that season, failed contract talks led him to free agency, and Maddux signed with the Atlanta Braves. He spent the next 11 seasons with the Braves, making the Cubs look bad every moment of his stay.

During spring training in 2004, Maddux signed a free-agent deal to return to the Cubs. He was supposed to be their fifth starter but matched Carlos Zambrano with the team lead in victories at 16. On August 7 that season, he earned his 300th career victory.

From 1988 through 2004, Maddux became the first pitcher to have 17 consecutive seasons with 15 or more victories. Phil Favia, a former scout for the Montreal Expos and Los Angeles Dodgers, said it best years ago: "Maddux is so good, we all should be wearing tuxedos when he pitches."

MADDUX

300

ARAMIS
RAMIREZ

92

Making a run at the National League Central title in 2003, the Cubs beefed up before the July 31 trading deadline, acquiring from the Pittsburgh Pirates Kenny Lofton as a short-term fix in the leadoff spot and Aramis Ramirez as a long-term solution to the black hole that had become third base.

Remember, since Ron Santo's departure after the 1973 season, the Cubs had started 97 different players at third, including 18 different starters on Opening Day, before Ramirez arrived.

Cubs general manager Jim Hendry was intrigued by Ramirez's strong showing his first full season in the majors, hitting .300 with 34 home runs and 112 RBI in 2001. Ramirez's average slipped to .234 and his homers dropped to 18 the next season, so this would be a project.

Ramirez helped lift the Cubs into the playoffs in 2003, hitting 15 home runs in 63 games. His 33 errors that season at third base, however, were a major concern.

With help from veterans Moises Alou and Sammy Sosa, Ramirez became a more focused player in Chicago. In 2004, he returned to his 2001 form, hitting .318 with 36 home runs and 103 RBI.

Looks like the Cubs solved their problem at third base.

RON
SANTO

A generation of Cubs fans have known Ron Santo as the passionate radio voice of the team on WGN. But as a player, he put together a Hall of Fame-caliber career at third base.

A nine-time All-Star, Santo won five consecutive Gold Gloves at third base from 1964 through '68. On September, 28, 2003, the Cubs retired Santo's jersey No. 10 as he joined Ernie Banks (14) and Billy Williams (26) to have their jersey numbers retired (Ryne Sandberg's No. 23 was retired in 2005, after his induction into the Hall of Fame). Seeing his No. 10 fly at Wrigley is what Santo calls his Hall of Fame.

Each year, he inches closer to Cooperstown, only to be disappointed. Santo hit more than 23 homers in eight seasons, belting a career-best 33 in 1965. But the Cubs lost 90 games that year and finished in eighth place. It's that kind of history that has hurt Santo in the eyes of Hall of Famer voters.

Offensively, Santo compares favorably to American League contemporary Brooks Robinson, the slick-fielding third baseman of the Baltimore Orioles. Both players operated in an era ruled by pitchers. What separates these two is their work in the postseason. Robinson hit .303 with five home runs and 22 RBI in 39 postseason games. He was the World Series MVP in 1970, hitting .429 and putting on an astonishing show at third base that secured his spot as a first-ballot Hall of Famer.

Santo had zero at-bats in the postseason—the true curse of playing for the Cubs from 1960 through '73 and the White Sox in 1974.

Traded by the Cincinnati Reds with Frank Baumholtz to the Cubs for Harry Walker and Peanuts Lowrey on June 15, 1949, Hank Sauer soon became "Mayor of Wrigley Field."

He played during one of the toughest stretches for the Cubs—leaving after the 1955 season without a single season with a winning record—but "The Honker" gave fans a reason to come to the ballpark. Fans showered the big-nosed, slow-footed outfielder with packets of chewing tobacco whenever he returned to his left field position following a blast over the wall.

Sauer's best season came in 1952, when his 37 home runs and 121 RBI were tops in the National League. He became the first player from a second-division team—the Cubs went 77–77 to finish in fifth place—to win the MVP Award. Two years later, playing for a 64–90 Cubs team as a 37-year-old, Sauer nearly matched his MVP performance, hitting .288 with 41 homers and 103 RBI.

Sauer retired and later became a scout for the San Francisco Giants. He died—at the age of 84— after teeing off on the first hole of a Bay Area golf course and suffering a massive heart attack.

HANK

SAUER

97

ALFONSO SORIANO

Alfonso Soriano's professional baseball career began in 1997—in Japan. The next season, he was playing for the New York Yankees. Soriano soon proved to be a deadly leadoff hitter, and by 2003, he set the major-league record for most home runs to lead off a game in a season with 13.

But Yankees owner George Steinbrenner was concerned about Soriano's defense. When the Yankees had the chance to get Alex Rodriguez from the Texas Rangers before the 2004 season, they decided to part with Soriano. By 2006, Soriano was with the Washington Nationals, playing left field for the first time. And he flexed his offensive muscle, putting up a 40–40–40 season—46 homers, 41 doubles and 41 stolen bases.

The Cubs, during a massive rebuilding effort after a 96-loss season in 2006, made Soriano the key piece of their makeover. During a lunch visit at the general managers' meetings with GM Jim Hendry and new manager Lou Piniella, Soriano agreed to an eight-year, $136 million contract.

The Cubs had the leadoff hitter they had been craving. During his first season on the North Side, Soriano broke Rick Monday's franchise record of eight home runs to lead off a game, set in 1976.

Sammy Sosa came to the Cubs during a late spring-training trade with the White Sox in 1992 as a five-tool star with plenty of potential. During a 13-year stay on the North Side, Sosa belted 545 home runs as a Cub. He called the 1998 home run chase with Mark McGwire the highlight of his career. Sosa smacked 66 homers, finishing second in the chase to McGwire's 70 for the rival St. Louis Cardinals.

That year was the first of Sosa's unmatched three seasons with 60 or more home runs. He soon replaced announcer Harry Caray as the main attraction at Wrigley Field, becoming a fan favorite. But things began to sour in 2003, when during a game against Lou Piniella's Tampa Bay Devil Rays at Wrigley, Sosa's bat shattered, exposing cork inside.

The split with Chicago became official during the final game of the 2004 season, shortly after the Cubs had squandered their lead in the wild-card chase. Sosa left Wrigley Field early, walking away from the team. He was traded to the Baltimore Orioles the following February.

After taking the 2006 season off, Sosa returned to baseball in 2007, signing with his original team, the Texas Rangers. On June 20, 2007, he became the fifth player in major-league history to reach 600 home runs—hitting the milestone homer against the Cubs. The pitcher was Jason Marquis, wearing Sosa's old No. 21 jersey.

SAMMY
SOSA

HIPPO VAUGHN

James Leslie "Hippo" Vaughn got his nickname thanks to a frame as big as his home state of Texas.

In nine seasons with the Cubs (1913–21), the 6-foot-4, 215-pound left-hander won 20 games five times, including a career-high 23 in 1917. One of his main claims to fame is somewhat dubious, though still impressive—especially by today's standards.

On May 2, 1917, Vaughn took the loss in baseball's only double no-hitter. Facing the Cincinnati Reds at Wrigley Field, Vaughn and right-hander Fred Toney—a 6-foot-6, 245-pound bulldog—were locked in a classic pitchers' duel. The game's first hit came in the 10th inning, when the Reds started a winning rally. Toney kept the Cubs hitless in the bottom of the inning to secure his no-hit victory.

The next season, Vaughn won the triple crown for pitchers, leading the National League in wins (22), ERA (1.74) and strikeouts (148).

BILLY RON ERNIE
WILLIAMS SANTO BANKS

The Chicago Cubs' finest trio: Billy Williams, Ron Santo, and Ernie Banks. Arguably the most popular players in franchise history, this nucleus of sluggers led the attack from 1961 through '71, blasting more than 1,200 home runs and tallying more than 4,200 RBI. The stellar trio made a combined total of 17 All-Star appearances.

Always entertaining, always fiery, Carlos Zambrano became the Cubs' ace in 2004—the problem was, no one really noticed until three years later, when it was clear neither Kerry Wood nor Mark Prior was the best pitcher in the rotation.

After going 13–11 with a 3.11 ERA during the Cubs' run to the 2003 National League Championship Series, Zambrano showed he had finally emerged from the shadow cast by Wood and Prior in 2004, going 16–8 with a 2.75 ERA.

An imposing right-hander who stands 6–5 and weighs 255 pounds, Zambrano is one of baseball's fiercest competitors on the field. His emotions got the best of him on June 1, 2007, when he got into a dugout shoving match with Cubs catcher Michael Barrett. The two later squared off in the clubhouse, and Big Z sent his catcher to the hospital with a black eye and in need of stitches in his lip.

Keeping Z's emotions in check has always been a challenge for the Cubs, but they knew they had a bona-fide ace and kept him off the free-agent mark in August 2007 by signing him to a five-year, $91.5 million contract extension.

CAP ANSON
FRANK CHANCE
JOE MCCARTHY
GABBY HARTNETT
CHARLIE GRIMM
LEO DUROCHER
JIM FREY
DON ZIMMER
DUSTY BAKER
LOU PINIELLA

4

CLASSIC
Cubs

THE MANAGERS

CAP ANSON

His plaque hanging in the first-floor gallery at the National Baseball Hall of Fame says it all about Adrian Constantine "Cap" Anson: "Greatest hitter and greatest National League player-manager of 19th century."

A star player with 3,081 hits on his résumé—though a butcher at first base—Anson was also a crafty player/manager for the Chicago White Stockings, or Colts, guiding the team to five NL pennants, including three straight from 1880 through '82, and 1,283 victories.

He was one of the first managers to rely on the stolen base and helped create the hit-and-run play as an offensive weapon. He also is credited with devising the first pitching rotation.

Through tours of England and other points in Europe during the late 1880s, Anson helped promote baseball on a worldwide scale, but he was one of the game's biggest bigots when it came to allowing black players in the major leagues. He is said to have pulled his team off the field when the opposing team had a black player on its squad.

Anson, who eventually became a part owner of the White Stockings, left the Chicago team after the 1897 season and managed the New York Giants for 22 games the next season.

FRANK
CHANCE

Frank Chance first gained the attention of Cubs fans as the first baseman in the famed "Tinker-to-Evers-to-Chance" double-play combination in the first decade of the 20th century. Just 27 when he replaced Frank Selee during the 1905 season, Chance quickly evolved into a respected player/manager.

Tabbed "The Peerless Leader," Chance led the Cubs to National League pennants in 1906, '07, '08, and '10, and won World Series titles in 1907 and '08. His first full season managing, the Cubs won a record 116 games in 1906. His intense nature landed him a spot in history—becoming the first player ever ejected from a World Series game, when he got the thumb during Game 3 of the 1910 Series against the Philadelphia Athletics.

Chance helped build a Cubs dynasty, and when his team finished third in 1912—a year after a surprising second-place finish—he was fired, much to the dismay of loyal fans. Chance was hired by the New York Yankees in 1913, but his career took a steep downturn. His first losing season as a player/manager was 1913, and during another losing effort, he was fired in 1914. He finished his major-league managerial career with a one-year stint guiding the last-place Boston Red Sox in 1923.

JOE McCARTHY

A career minor-leaguer as a player, Joe McCarthy made his mark as one of the greatest managers in major-league history.

Coming off a last-place finish in 1925, the Cubs gave McCarthy his first major-league managerial job in 1926. He quickly raised hopes, guiding the Cubs to an 82–72 record, good enough for fourth place. By 1929—behind a steady rise in victories each season on the job—he ended the Cubs' 11-year World Series drought by guiding them to a National League pennant and a $10\frac{1}{2}$-game cushion.

As a Philadelphia native, he grew up idolizing Connie Mack, and faced Mr. Mack's Athletics in the World Series, where the Cubs were sent home in five games—after blowing leads in Games 4 and 5. With four games left in the 1930 season—and the Cubs headed to a second-place finish—owner William Wrigley Jr. fired McCarthy and replaced him with Rogers Hornsby.

McCarthy was snatched up by the New York Yankees and, in his second year at the helm, guided them to the 1932 World Series. That's where he got his revenge on the Cubs, knocking them off in four games. That was the first of six World Series titles with the Yankees for McCarthy, who became the first manager to capture pennants in both leagues. McCarthy's .614 winning percentage remains the highest in baseball history.

Tabbed "The Perfect Catcher" by Cubs manager Joe McCarthy, Hartnett was considered the best backstop during the first half of the 20th century. In the middle of the 1938 season, Charlie Grimm resigned as Cubs manager, saying he could no longer control his players. Hartnett was tabbed to replace his friend—and former teammate—who moved into the broadcast booth.

As player/manager, Hartnett took over on July 20, with the Cubs in third-place, trailing the league-leading Pittsburgh Pirates by $5\frac{1}{2}$ games. Under Hartnett, the Cubs went 44–27 the rest of the way to claim the pennant. It wasn't an easy ride. By August 31, they were in fourth place, seven games out. But Hartnett's Cubs went 22–7–2 in September, helped by his "Homer in the Gloamin'"—a dramatic tiebreaking home run by the player/manager against the Pirates at Wrigley Field on September 28.

The Cubs were swept out of the World Series by the Yankees. It marked the fourth time in 10 years the Cubs were knocked off in the Fall Classic. Grimm was fired two years later, on the heels of a fifth-place finish and a 79–70 run in 1940—his only losing season as manager.

GABBY
HARTNETT

CHARLIE GRIMM

A respected fielder as a first baseman during his 20-year playing career, Charlie Grimm was tapped to be the Cubs' player/manager late in the 1932 season as the players grew tired of Rogers Hornsby's heavy-handed approach.

"Jolly Cholly" definitely had the right touch for these Cubs. When he took over on August 2, the Cubs were in second place, five games behind the Pirates. Helped by a 14-game winning streak in September, they won the pennant but were swept by the Yankees in the World Series. He guided them to another pennant in 1935 thanks to a 21-game winning streak that September.

Famous for being a "players' manager," Grimm stepped down in the middle of the 1938 season, saying he couldn't control or relate to his players. He returned to the Cubs early in the 1944 season. The next season, he took them to the 1945 World Series, the last before the club's famous drought. He was fired during the 1949 season but summoned back—from the broadcast booth—for a final 17-game run with the Cubs during the 1960 season.

After Grimm died in 1983—at 85 and while still serving as an assistant to then-general manager Dallas Green—his widow received permission to spread "Jolly Cholly's" ashes at Wrigley Field.

Coining phrases such as "Nice guys finish last," and 'Show me a good loser and I'll show you an idiot," Leo Durocher was one of the most passionate managers in baseball history.

After stints with the Brooklyn Dodgers and New York Giants—and an 11-year layoff—Durocher came to the Cubs at the end of their managerial experiment known as the "College of Coaches." At his introductory news conference in 1966, "Leo the Lip" made clear his job title. "I'm not a head coach," Durocher said. "I'm the manager."

With just two winning seasons the previous 20 years, the Cubs had high hopes for Durocher, but his 1966 debut was a huge disappointment as the team lost 103 games and finished in 10th place.

But Durocher's 1969 Cubs offered up an even bigger disappointment. Playing in the newly aligned National League East, the Cubs were in first place for 103 days. By August 14, they enjoyed an $9\frac{1}{2}$-game lead over the third-place New York Mets. Sunk by an eight-game losing streak in early September, the Cubs stumbled down the stretch. When the dust settled, they finished in second place, eight games behind the Mets.

The fiery manager had regular run-ins with stars Ernie Banks and Ron Santo and was fired midway through the 1972 season, having never led the Cubs to the postseason.

LEO DUROCHER

JIM FREY

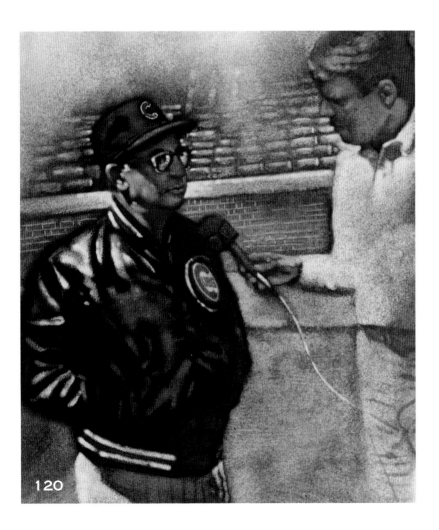

When he got his first major-league managerial job, Jim Frey took the Kansas City Royals to their first World Series during his rookie season of 1980. But he was fired before the end of the next season after his in-game judgment came under fire.

Frey's next major-league managerial job came with the Cubs in 1984, and again, he enjoyed instant success, guiding them to their first postseason appearance since 1945. During his first spring training as Cubs manager, Frey had a huge impact on the career of future Hall of Famer Ryne Sandberg, sidling up to the second baseman during spring training and giving him the green light to swing for the fences. That put Sandberg on the path to an MVP season.

His eye for talent was Frey's strongest suit. He was fired two months into the 1986 season. In 1987, Frey was hired to do color commentary on WGN Radio, but by the end of that season, the Cubs hired Frey to replace his boss, general manager Dallas Green. Relying on his talent-evaluating skills, Frey made a series of bold moves from the front office that helped the Cubs win a division title in 1989.

A scrappy infielder during his playing days, Don Zimmer's career took a scary turn in 1953 when—while leading the American Association in home runs—he was beaned at the plate and spent 13 days in a coma.

He bounced back and was captain of the Cubs in 1961, the first year of P. K. Wrigley's ill-fated College of Coaches. "Popeye"—a vocal critic of the College of Coaches—was an All-Star second baseman that season, and his own future career as a manager clearly wasn't tarnished by the bad idea.

General manager Jim Frey hired his old high school pal from Cincinnati to manage the Cubs in 1988. His second season at the helm, Zimmer guided the Cubs to the National League East title, relying on a few unorthodox moves—including some bases-loaded squeeze plays—and a makeshift roster to win 93 games.

But once in the NL Championship Series, every one of Zimmer's moves seemed to fizzle. Fans and media turned on him as the San Francisco Giants knocked off the Cubs in five games.

After a fourth-place finish in 1990 and a slow start the next season, Zimmer issued an ultimatum less than two months into 1991 season: he wanted to know his fate by July 1. The Cubs fired him on May 21.

DUSTY BAKER

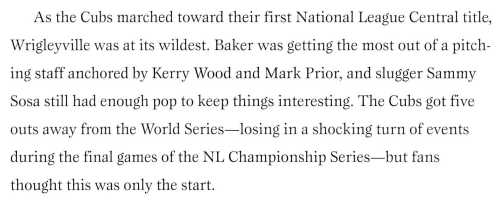

After taking the San Francisco Giants to the 2002 World Series, Dusty Baker seemed a long-shot candidate to take the Cubs' vacant managerial job. But general manager Jim Hendry kept courting Baker through the World Series and got his man after Baker's bitter split with San Francisco.

Baker immediately went on a campaign to change the Cubs' culture, spouting catch phrases such as "Why not us?" and squashing any mention of the "Lovable Losers." Midway through his first season in 2003, fans were believers, wearing "In Dusty We Trusty" T-shirts.

As the Cubs marched toward their first National League Central title, Wrigleyville was at its wildest. Baker was getting the most out of a pitching staff anchored by Kerry Wood and Mark Prior, and slugger Sammy Sosa still had enough pop to keep things interesting. The Cubs got five outs away from the World Series—losing in a shocking turn of events during the final games of the NL Championship Series—but fans thought this was only the start.

Instead, 2003 was the pinnacle of the Baker years. The Cubs never returned to the playoffs—despite having a reloaded roster for 2004—and Baker was fired the day after the final game of the 2006 season when the Cubs lost 96 games to finish in last place.

LOU PINIELLA

On Lou Piniella's first day as the 48th manager in Cubs history—October 17, 2007—he got tripped up by goats, curses, and geography. He referred to the White Sox as the North Siders and called the Magnificent Mile shopping district the Michigan Mile.

But he did mention the ivy and the Bleacher Bums. And he put all of that history surrounding the Cubs—nearly a century's worth of it being mostly bad news—in its proper perspective. "They hire managers to win; there is no other reason."

And that's what Piniella did. After Dusty Baker was dismissed on the heels of a 96-loss season in 2006, Piniella came in and enjoyed every bit of the Cubs' $300 million off-season spending spree. The ride was bumpy at first, with players bristling over Piniella's in-your-face style. The days of Baker coddling his players were over.

But by June—after Piniella's famous dirt-kicking tirade to take the focus away from a dugout scuffle the day before between ace Carlos Zambrano and catcher Michael Barrett—the Cubs had found their winning ways, marching toward the National League Central title.

Piniella set out to do what he accomplished with the Cincinnati Reds in 1990—win a World Series his first year in town.

1906 WORLD SERIES

1907 WORLD SERIES

1908 WORLD SERIES

BABE RUTH'S CALLED SHOT

HOMER IN THE GLOAMIN'

THE BILLY GOAT CURSE

COLLEGE OF COACHES

1969 COLLAPSE

LEE ELIA'S TIRADE

THE SANDBERG GAME

1984 PLAYOFFS

KERRY WOOD'S 20-K GAME

2005 – FIVE OUTS AWAY

5

CLASSIC Cubs

GREAT ... AND NOT SO GREAT

MOMENTS

This was a mismatch on a grand scale: the "Hitless Wonders" White Sox, who finished with an American League-worst .230 team batting average, against the mighty Cubs, who won a staggering 116 games, which would go on as the most ever during the 154-game era.

Even if the Cubs were heavily favored, Chicago was loving the moment. This was the first World Series to feature two teams from the same city, and in true Chicago fashion, snow flurries were part of the pregame ceremonies for Game 1 at the Cubs' West Side Grounds.

The "Hitless Wonders" lived up to their name, combining for a .198 average during the World Series. That was to be expected against a Cubs team that boasted a 1.76 team ERA during the regular season. But the Sox' .198 mark actually bettered the Cubs' average of .196 in the Series.

In a desperation move on the brink of elimination in Game 6, Cubs manager Frank Chance started Mordecai "Three-Finger" Brown on one day of rest and paid dearly. In the second inning, the Sox chased Brown, who had no-hit them into the sixth inning and allowed just two hits in a Game 4 victory. Brown yielded seven runs and eight hits, and the Sox rolled to a Series-clinching 8–3 victory.

1906 WORLD SERIES

1907
WORLD SERIES

The best way to erase the bitterness of the 1906 World Series was to return to the Fall Classic the next season and put on a dominant performance. That's the formula followed by the 1907 Cubs, who swept the Detroit Tigers in four games.

But this Series actually featured five games—the first a rainout that ended in a tie. The tied Game 1 gets somewhat lost in history, but it set the stage for the Cubs' sweep.

In a pitchers' duel, the Cubs carried a 1–0 lead into the eighth inning, but the Tigers staged a three-run rally in the eighth and appeared to be ready to put the game away. Facing Tigers right-hander Wild Bill Donovan, who was 25–4 in the regular season, the Cubs staged their own late rally, scoring two runs in the ninth to force extra innings.

Even in the ninth, the Tigers had a chance to close out the victory when Del Howard struck out with two outs. But Tigers catcher Charlie Schmidt couldn't hold on to strike three, and the tying run scored. The pitchers took over from there, keeping it 3–3 until darkness forced the game to be called after 12 innings.

That momentum shift helped push the Cubs to a sweep of the next four games and their first World Series title.

1908 WORLD SERIES

As strange as it sounds today, the Cubs were becoming baseball's first dynasty by 1908. They waltzed through the 1906 season, only to be shocked by the White Sox in the World Series. They put on a dominant performance to sweep the Detroit Tigers in the 1907 Series. And they were on baseball's biggest stage the next fall—facing the Tigers in the first World Series rematch.

Reaching this Series was probably as exciting as the World Series itself. The Cubs needed a one-game play-off against the New York Giants to reach the postseason. The playoff was actually a makeup of a September 23 game against the New York Giants that ended in a tie at the Polo Grounds. That game featured a legendary play: Merkle's boner.

The Giants were rallying in the bottom of the ninth of a tie game. Moose McCormick was on third base, and 19-year-old Fred Merkle was on first with two outs. Al Bridwell singled and fans stormed the field. Merkle never reached second, thinking the game was over. But Cubs second baseman Johnny Evers noticed Merkle's lapse, retrieved a ball—which may or may not have been the game ball—touched second, and Merkle was forced out, nullifying the run and keeping the score tied.

Darkness forced the game to be made up at the end of the season. The Cubs won the makeup and finished one game ahead of the Giants to face the Tigers in the World Series.

This Series victory would have to hold Cubs fans over for a while as the longest championship drought in major-league baseball history was about to begin.

BABE RUTH'S
CALLED SHOT

One of the most talked-about home runs ever hit at Wrigley Field came during the 1932 World Series against the New York Yankees.

Tension had been building between Yankees slugger Babe Ruth and the Cubs. Ruth was angry at the Cubs for voting only a half postseason share to his former teammate Mark Koenig and had been ripping the North Siders in the papers. Things came to a head before Game 3 of the Series, after the first two games had been played at Yankee Stadium. Getting abuse from the Cubs as he took batting practice, Ruth turned to their dugout and reportedly shouted: "Hey, you damn bum Cubs, you won't be seeing Yankee Stadium again. This is going to be all over Sunday."

When he came to bat in the fifth inning, the Babe already had a three-run homer under his belt. He was still getting abuse from the Cubs' bench and fans in the stands. After strike one from Cubs pitcher Charlie Root, Ruth rose one finger in the air and yelled, "Strike one." He displayed two fingers after strike two. According to legend, before a 2–2 pitch, Ruth pointed—either at Root, the Cubs' bench, or right-center field, depending on who is telling the story.

Ruth swung from his heels and deposited the ball well beyond the right-center wall.

Gabby Hartnett hit 236 home runs during a Hall of Fame career, but none was bigger than his shot on September 28, 1938, at Wrigley Field.

It would be nearly 50 years before Wrigley Field would get lights when Hartnett—the Cubs' player/manager—stepped to the plate with none on and two outs in the ninth inning of a 5–5 game against the Pittsburgh Pirates. With the sun setting and an odd haze smothering Wrigley, fans couldn't see most of the field. The umpires had already decided this would be the last inning, with the game resuming the following day.

Pirates pitcher Bob Klinger put Hartnett into an 0–2 hole. His next pitch was clobbered by Hartnett, who sent it into the left-field seats, giving the Cubs a 6–5 victory on the "Homer in the Gloamin'."

The Pirates, who entered the game with a half-game lead, were stunned. Three days later, the Cubs clinched the pennant, capping an amazing late-season rally.

Hartnett, by the way, was behind the plate for one of the other most famous home runs at Wrigley Field—Babe Ruth's "Called Shot" during the 1932 World Series.

HOMER IN THE GLOAMIN'

THE BILLY GOAT
CURSE

It was Game 4 of the 1945 World Series between the Detroit Tigers and the Cubs, and Chicago tavern owner William "Billy Goat" Sianis arrived at Wrigley Field with two tickets, one for himself and one for his mascot—a live goat named Murphy.

Sianis and his goat were allowed into the ballpark and reportedly paraded around the field before the game. When Sianis tried to settle into his box seats—goat in tow—fans complained. Eventually, Cubs owner P. K. Wrigley ordered ushers to remove Sianis from the stadium, saying the goat's odor was offensive to paying customers.

Sianis was irate and, according to legend, placed a curse on the Cubs that they never again would reach the World Series. The Cubs lost that game and got knocked out by the Tigers in seven games of the '45 Fall Classic. While vacationing in Greece, Sianis supposedly sent a nasty note to Wrigley, asking: "Who stinks now?"

The curse supposedly was lifted by Sianis shortly before his death in 1969. The curse was back four years later, though. William Sianis's nephew Sam, who inherited the family's Billy Goat Tavern, arrived at Wrigley Field on July 4, 1973, to celebrate the Cubs' spot in first place. But Sam Sianis and his goat, Socrates, were turned away, and the hex was back on.

P K WRIGLEY

presents the

COLLEGE of COACHES

ALL NEW
for 1961!

SEE THE EXCITEMENT OF "ROTATING" MANAGERS!

Wrigley Field Clark and Addison Streets

One of the worst decisions in Cubs history was a by-product of a failed contract negotiation. After the 1960 season, owner P. K. Wrigley was locked in a battle with manager Lou Boudreau, who was seeking a two-year contract.

Wrigley wasn't sold. He looked up the word *manager* in the dictionary and claimed the definition was "dictator." This didn't sit well with Wrigley, who preferred a more democratic rule by his coaching staff. So he granted equal authority to each of his coaches—Vedie Himsl, Harry Craft, El Tappe, and Lou Klein—for the 1961 season. The Cubs went 64–90, but Wrigley wasn't ready to abandon the plan.

In 1962, the "College of Coaches" consisted of Tappe, Klein, and Charlie Metro, and the Cubs went 59–103. Wrigley's plan was derided as a failed innovation, but it had some merit. His original plan called for eight coaches to rotate through the entire organization, preaching a consistent style of baseball, getting players to play the Cubs' way. But players got confused by all of the bosses, and the coaches—who had trouble hiding their jealousy—didn't work well together.

By 1963, the Cubs were back to one manager, Bob Kennedy, and went a more respectable 82–80.

CUBS

Lou Brock TRADED Outfield

It was a one-sided trade from the first second it was announced on June 15, 1964. The St. Louis Cardinals were dealing 28-year-old pitcher Ernie Broglio—a 60-game winner from 1960 to '63—to the Cubs for Lou Brock, a 24-year-old undisciplined hitter who struck out a lot and didn't seem to have the proper instincts on the bases.

What were the Cardinals thinking?

It was, indeed, a lopsided deal—the worst trade in Cubs history.

At the time of the trade, Brock was hitting .251, with two

home runs and 14 RBI in 52 games. Broglio was 3–5 but had a respectable 3.50 ERA in 11 starts for the Cards. Everything changed after the trade. Brock hit .348, stole 33 bases, and paced the Cardinals to a World Series victory—on the way to a Hall of Fame career.

As for Broglio, he went 4–7 for the Cubs in 1964, following that with a 1–6 mark in 1965 and a 2–6 record before retiring after the 1966 season.

In a fitting twist, Brock became the 14th player in baseball history—and only the second Cardinal at the time—to bag his 3,000th hit, doing so on August 13, 1979, against the Cubs.

1969
COLLAPSE

In the baseball world, this was the very definition of sitting pretty: August 14, 1969, and the Cubs are in first place, $8\frac{1}{2}$ games ahead of the second-place St. Louis Cardinals and $9\frac{1}{2}$ games ahead of the third-place New York Mets.

As Mets outfielder Cleon Jones said of the Cubs: "They were already starting to count that 25 grand [in playoff money]."

Maybe it was all that day baseball and the steamy weather at Wrigley Field, but the Cubs were running out of gas by early September, when they went on an eight-game losing streak. Players point back to a July 8 game against the Mets at Shea Stadium as a sign of bad things to come. A black cat scampered across the field, right in front of the Cubs' dugout. For a team that believed in curses, that certainly seemed like one.

Down the stretch, the Cubs went 14–20 while the Amazin' Mets got on a 23–7 roll. When the dust settled, the Mets had finished in first place, eight games ahead of the second-place Cubs.

Manager Leo Durocher best summed up the Cubs' colossal collapse of 1969 by saying: "I could have dressed nine broads up as ballplayers, and they would have beaten the Cubs."

I'll tell you one f*ckin' thing, I hope we get f*ckin' hotter than sh*t, just to stuff it up them 3,000 f*ckin' people that show up every f*ckin' day, because if they're the real Chicago f*ckin' fans, they can kiss my f*ckin' ass

right downtown

and PRINT IT!

We're mired now in a little difficulty, ...are f*ckin' fans who come out here and say they're Cub fans that are ...supposed to be behind you, rippin' every f*ckin' thing you do.

...he motherf*ckers don't even work. That's why they're out at the f*ckin' game. They oughta go out and get a f*ckin' job and find ...t what it's like to go out and earn a f*ckin' living.

Eighty-five percent of the f*ckin' world is working. The other fifteen percent come out here.

Five consecutive losing seasons and a 5–14 start to the 1983 season were taking a toll on the Cubs and their fiery second-year manager, Lee Elia. The negativity surrounding Wrigley Field is hard to imagine these days. For Elia—in April 1983—it was hard to escape.

So he finally snapped.

Elia was trying to stick up for his team of rising stars, a group that included future Hall of Famer Ryne Sandberg playing his first full season at second base. Elia was angry when a crowd of 9.391 on a Friday afternoon showed its displeasure after the Los Angeles Dodgers snapped a 3–3 tie in the eighth when Ken Landreaux scored the winning run on a wild pitch by Cubs reliever Lee Smith.

During a three-minute tirade to reporters, Elia spewed 448 words—most of them unprintable.

"We got guys bustin' their [bleeping] ass, and them [bleeping] people boo," Elia said. "And that's the Cubs? That's what my players get around here? . . . If they're the real Chicago [bleeping] fans, they can kiss my [bleeping bleep] right downtown. And print it. Print it!

"Eighty-five percent of the [bleeping] world's working. The other 15 come out here."

Later that day—thanks to some fast damage control by general manager Dallas Green—Elia apologized. That delayed his firing, until August.

THE
SANDBERG GAME

GAME OF THE WEEK

NBC

148

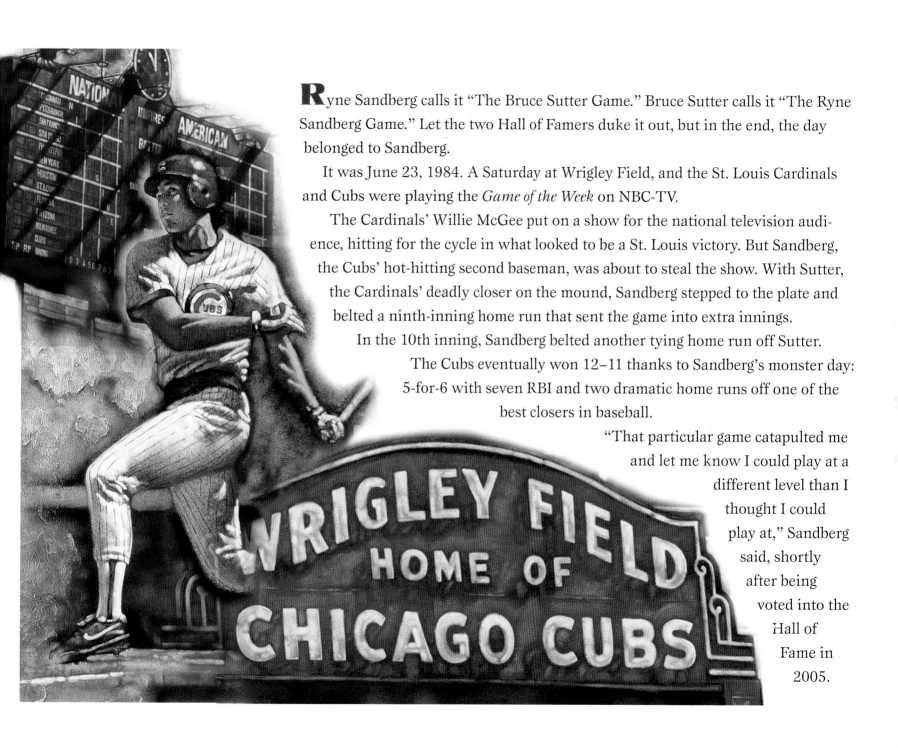

Ryne Sandberg calls it "The Bruce Sutter Game." Bruce Sutter calls it "The Ryne Sandberg Game." Let the two Hall of Famers duke it out, but in the end, the day belonged to Sandberg.

It was June 23, 1984. A Saturday at Wrigley Field, and the St. Louis Cardinals and Cubs were playing the *Game of the Week* on NBC-TV.

The Cardinals' Willie McGee put on a show for the national television audience, hitting for the cycle in what looked to be a St. Louis victory. But Sandberg, the Cubs' hot-hitting second baseman, was about to steal the show. With Sutter, the Cardinals' deadly closer on the mound, Sandberg stepped to the plate and belted a ninth-inning home run that sent the game into extra innings.

In the 10th inning, Sandberg belted another tying home run off Sutter.

The Cubs eventually won 12–11 thanks to Sandberg's monster day: 5-for-6 with seven RBI and two dramatic home runs off one of the best closers in baseball.

"That particular game catapulted me and let me know I could play at a different level than I thought I could play at," Sandberg said, shortly after being voted into the Hall of Fame in 2005.

1984
PLAYOFFS

For the first time since the 1945 World Series, the Cubs were in the postseason, facing the San Diego Padres in the 1984 National League Championship Series—then a best-of-five affair.

Chicago could sense a World Series was on the horizon after the Cubs opened a 2–0 lead in the series at Wrigley Field, including a 13–0 rout in Game 1 that showed the balance of power resided in the Midwest. When the NLCS moved to San Diego, the Cubs opened a 1–0 lead in Game 3, but the Padres rallied for a 7–1 victory. Game 4 was a seesaw battle that ended with Steve Garvey's two-run homer in the bottom of the ninth, forcing a Game 5 in San Diego.

The Cubs jumped to a 3–0 lead and had ace Rick Sutcliffe on the mound. He delivered five scoreless innings before allowing two runs in the sixth. With one out in the seventh and a runner on second base, Padres pinch hitter Tim Flannery hit a routine grounder to first baseman Leon Durham. Easy out—until the ball rolled through Durham's legs, allowing the tying run to score and opening the door to a four-run Padres seventh.

No Cubs slide would be complete without an intriguing back story. According to legend, Cubs second baseman Ryne Sandberg spilled Gatorade on Durham's glove in a dugout accident shortly before the pivotal play.

KERRY WOOD'S
20-K GAME

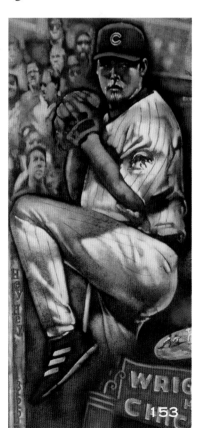

In the post-Greg Maddux days of the late 1990s, fireballing right-hander Kerry Wood was tabbed as the next big thing on the mound for the Cubs. During his Rookie of the Year season in 1998, Wood lived up to the billing and won Cubs fans over with one monster outing.

It was May 6, 1998, and the Houston Astros were at Wrigley Field. When Wood first stepped on the mound that day, he was 2–2—nothing flashy, but solid. In the first inning, the right-hander struck out the first three batters, then stopped counting. The fans in left field ran out of cardboard signs after 11 strikeouts and began painting K's on their chests. At one point, Wood struck out seven in a row. He entered the ninth inning having allowed one hit, a Ricky Gutierrez infield single in the third inning that glanced off the glove of third baseman Kevin Orie.

Wood had 18 strikeouts with three outs left. When pinch hitter Billy Spiers opened the ninth by striking out, Wood tied the National League single-game mark for K's. Leadoff hitter Craig Biggio grounded to short, disappointing the crowd of 15,758. Then Derek Bell went down swinging, giving Wood 20 strikeouts, matching Roger Clemens' major-league record.

Nearly eight years later, Biggio summed up the outing best: "Total dominance for a day."

Arm problems began to derail Wood's career by the end of his rookie season—but he will always have that one magical day.

FIVE OUTS AWAY

Dusty Baker's first year managing the Cubs, and 2003 seemed destined for a magical ending. The Cubs breezed past the Atlanta Braves in the first round of the playoffs and opened a 3–1 lead in the National League Championship Series against a young Florida Marlins team. Even after they dropped Game 5, the Cubs still enjoyed a comfortable advantage—going home for Games 6 and 7 with co-aces Mark Prior and Kerry Wood on tap.

The Cubs were five outs from stamping a World Series ticket in the eighth inning of Game 6. Plastic tarps had been tacked over the Cubs' lockers and champagne on ice was being wheeled into their clubhouse when everything fell apart.

After Prior retired Mike Mordecai on a fly ball, Juan Pierre doubled to left. Prior then got ahead of Luis Castillo 1–2 before falling behind 3–2. That's when Castillo fouled a ball down the left-field line. Moises Alou raced to the stands, reached over the railing—and watched in horror as a fan knocked the ball out of his glove.

Those believing in curses will blame spectator Steve Bartman for deflecting the foul ball. History shows shortstop Alex Gonzalez booted a routine grounder by Miguel Cabrera later in the inning that might have had more to do with Prior's unraveling. In the end, the Marlins rallied for eight runs in the eighth inning.

The Cubs still had a reasonable shot in Game 7, taking a 5–3 lead into the fifth inning, but a three-run fifth—capped by Marlins first baseman Derrek Lee's RBI single—ended the dream season.

WILLIAM HULBERT

ALBERT SPALDING

CHARLES MURPHY

CHARLES WEEGHMAN

WILLIAM WRIGLEY JR.

P. K. WRIGLEY

TRIBUNE COMPANY

6

CLASSIC
Cubs

THE OWNERS

WILLIAM HULBERT

Born just a few miles outside of Cooperstown, New York, William Hulbert purchased controlling interest in the Chicago White Stockings (soon to be Cubs) in 1875 and began forming the National League. By 1876, Hulbert's mission was simple: build the world's best baseball team.

He began this ambitious goal by luring Boston Red Stockings ace pitcher Al Spalding— an Illinois native—and Philadelphia Athletics hitting sensation Adrian "Cap" Anson to join the first crop of talented players to defect to Chicago. The White Stockings won the first NL pennant, going 52–14 over their 66-game schedule.

But on April 10, 1882, Hulbert died of a heart attack at 49, and Spalding assumed club ownership—a stake he would hold for the next 20 years. Spalding credited Hulbert with saving the game of baseball by creating the National League.

The National Baseball Hall of Fame's veteran's committee—in a long overdue move— voted Hulbert into Cooperstown in 1995.

Hulbert is buried in Graceland Cemetery in Chicago, just down Clark Street from Wrigley Field. His grave is marked by a granite baseball honoring the formation of the NL.

ALBERT SPALDING

Baseball's first 200-game winner, Spalding guided the Chicago White Stockings to the National League pennant in 1876, winning 47 games as a pitcher and serving as its 26-year-old manager. His playing and managing career ended the next season.

Spalding, who grew up in Rockford, Illinois, then showed he knew a thing or two about the business side of the sport, forming his own sporting goods business that would help build the game on a global level.

Spalding took over ownership of the Cubs in 1882, immediately after the shocking death of owner William Hulbert, and guided the club to three pennants through 1902. His first order of business was to maintain Hulbert's pioneering ways, going on a decade-long crusade to rid the game of seedy gamblers and rid the ballparks of rowdy drinkers.

He also used his clout to attract star players to take baseball's first world tour, playing exhibitions in New Zealand, Australia, Ceylon (now Sri Lanka), Egypt, Italy, France, and England during an 1888–89 trek that included welcome-home receptions in New York, Philadelphia, and Chicago.

Spalding was inducted into the National Baseball Hall of Fame in 1939 as a pioneer and executive.

161

CHARLES
MURPHY

A former baseball writer for the *Cincinnati Enquirer*, Charles W. Murphy was the Cubs' press agent when James Hart put the team on the market in 1905. In need of money, Murphy turned to Cincinnati businessman Charles Taft, brother of 27th U.S. President William Howard Taft, and secured the $105,000 needed to buy the team.

The next season, manager Frank Chance guided the Cubs to a 116–36 record, the best in major-league history. But the Cubs were knocked off by the White Sox in the 1906 World Series—the first to feature two teams from the same city. Murphy's Cubs returned to the Series in 1907 and quickly dispatched the Detroit Tigers.

The Cubs won their second World Series the next season, again beating the Tigers. But Murphy's successful early run as owner did little to inspire love from fans, who were irked by his high ticket prices for the Series.

Local legend has it that the night after the Cubs won the 1908 World Series, George M. Cohan, song-and-dance man of "Yankee Doodle Dandy" fame, threw a downtown party to honor the team—but purposely left Murphy off the invite list.

The snub is considered "the other curse" that plagued the Cubs over the next 100 years.

Two years after building a ballpark at the corner of Clark and Addison streets on the North Side for his Chicago Whales of the Federal League, Charles Weeghman led a group of investors who purchased the Cubs for $500,000 in 1916.

The Cubs immediately moved into Weeghman Park—now known as Wrigley Field—vacating the West Side Grounds, their beloved ballpark bordered by Taylor Street on the south, Polk Street on the north, Wolcott (then called Lincoln) on the west, and Wood Street on the east.

Famed Chicago sportswriter Ring Lardner condemned the Cubs' move to the North Side, writing on Opening Day 1916: "Now fades the glimmering landscape on the sight/Save for the chatter of the laboring folk/Returning to their hovels for the night/All is still at Taylor, Lincoln, Wood, and Polk. . . ."

"Lucky Charlie" Weeghman built his fortune off a successful lunch-counter chain of fast-food restaurants that popped up around the Chicago area. But when the chain went belly up, Weeghman was forced to sell controlling interest in his baseball team in 1921 to William Wrigley Jr., one of the original investors with his group.

CHARLES
WEEGHMAN

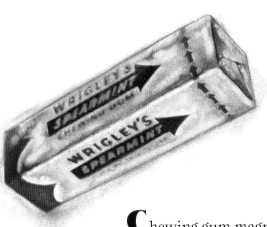

Chewing gum magnate William Wrigley Jr.—founder of the Wm. Wrigley Jr. Company—became the Cubs' owner in 1921 and kept the team in his family until 1981, making it the longest continuous operation of a franchise by one family in the same city.

Wrigley bought controlling interest in the team from Charles Weeghman. Their home at the corner of Clark and Addison was known as Weeghman Park until 1920, when it was called Cubs Park. After Wrigley ordered extensive expansion, the stadium was renamed Wrigley Field in 1926.

With a strong business presence in Southern California, Wrigley's top farm team was the Los Angeles Angels of the Pacific Coast League, and they also played in a ballpark called Wrigley Field.

During Wrigley's ownership, the Cubs moved their spring training to Avalon—the only city on Santa Catalina Island, some 20 miles off the Los Angeles coast—between 1922 and 1942, 1946–47, and 1950–51 because he owned controlling interest in the island.

Despite all of his business holdings, Wrigley perhaps valued the Cubs most. He held onto the team until his death in 1932, leaving the club to son P. K. Wrigley. Rumor has it his deathbed wish was that the team never be sold.

WILLIAM
WRIGLEY JR.

Philip Knight Wrigley, or P. K. to his friends, did not possess the same passion for the Cubs that his father, William Wrigley Jr., had shown during his tenure as owner.

The quieter P. K. Wrigley, who took over ownership when his father died in 1932, preferred to concentrate his energy on the family chewing-gum business, and the clan's hobby—the Cubs—suffered in the process.

During P. K.'s tenure, the Cubs won the pennant in 1932, '35, '38, and '45, but their World Series victory drought still stretched to 1908. Part of the lore of the 1945 World Series against the Detroit Tigers was the firing of Wrigley Field usher "One-Eyed" Connelly, who tried to prevent P. K. Wrigley from entering the park because he didn't have a ticket.

After the 1945 World Series, a long decline set in and Wrigley did little to reverse it, though he was a big proponent of televising his team's games free—on WGN-TV.

And P. K. did hold true to a supposed deathbed wish he granted his father—never to sell the Cubs—leaving the team to his son, William "Bill" Wrigley III, upon his death in 1977.

P. K. WRIGLEY

TRIBUNE COMPANY

Bill Wrigley brought his family's ownership of the Cubs, which began with a controlling interest in 1921, to an end 60 years later, selling the franchise and the ballpark to the Tribune Company for $20.5 million in 1981.

Despite a long-standing promise to keep the Cubs in the Wrigley fold, Bill Wrigley was forced to sell after both of his parents died within two months of each other in 1977, subjecting their $81 million estate to federal and state inheritance taxes.

In stepped the Tribune Company—owner of the *Chicago Tribune* newspaper, WGN-TV, and WGN Radio, among its media properties. The Tribune Company was interested because it was already broadcasting Cubs games on its radio station and cable superstation.

The media chain also took some progressive steps that had been resisted by the Wrigleys, notably installing lights at the team's ballpark. Bill Wrigley reportedly loved the idea of Wrigley Field being the only stadium in the majors without lights, and he wanted to preserve the Cubs' tradition of day games so players could spend evenings at home with their families.

Long considered penny-pinching for operating in such a large market, the Tribune Company spent big before the 2007 season, adding a crop of new players plus manager Lou Piniella during a $300 million shopping spree. In April 2007, the Tribune Company was purchased by real-estate tycoon Sam Zell, and the Cubs were immediately put on the market.

Hal Totten

Bob Elson

Bert Wilson

Jack Quinlan

Vince Lloyd

Lou Boudreau

Jack Brickhouse

Harry Caray

Pat Hughes

Ron Santo

Steve Stone

7

CLASSIC

Cubs

VOICES OF THE

GAME

HAL TOTTEN

A former rewrite man for the *Chicago Daily News*, 23-year-old Hal Totten was the first radio voice for the Cubs, teaming with Quin Ryan broadcasting games for WMAQ in 1924. That year, the Cubs and White Sox became the first two major-league teams to broadcast every home game.

The WMAQ deal helped spur interest in the Cubs, increasing attendance at Wrigley Field. Totten, with his monotone voice and dry sense of humor, continued his broadcasting career for 21 years, working into the early 1950s on Mutual Broadcasting System's *Game of the Day*—aired every day except Sunday.

One of his highlight moments was broadcasting Babe Ruth's "Called Shot" home run during the 1932 World Series at Wrigley Field. There was so much controversy over whether Ruth had actually called the home run, Totten asked him about it the next spring. Ruth shot down the tale, reportedly telling Totten: "Hell, no, I didn't point. Only a damned fool would do a thing like that. . . . I never really knew anybody who could tell you ahead of time where he was going to hit a baseball. When I get to be that kind of fool, they'll put me in a booby hatch."

BOB ELSON

Estimating he broadcast more than 5,000 baseball games, Bob Elson was known for his relaxed style during a 40-year career. The broadcasting pioneer is credited with conducting the first on-field interview, chatting with Philadelphia Athletics manager Connie Mack in 1931.

The Peoria native was lured away from St. Louis, where he earned his first radio job after winning a contest. WGN wanted him to broadcast Cubs and White Sox games in 1929, and a new era in Chicago broadcasting was under way. From 1930 to 1941, Elson was the radio voice for the Cubs.

Later in his career, Elson became known as "The Commander" because he enlisted in the Navy during World War II and rose to that rank during a four-year career. At the request of President Franklin D. Roosevelt—after some prodding from the Gillette Company—Elson was granted a two-week leave by the Navy to come home and broadcast the 1943 All-Star Game at Shibe Park in Philadelphia.

After the war, Elson returned to Chicago and spent the next 25 years broadcasting White Sox games. Elson left the White Sox after the 1970 season and spent 1971 broadcasting Oakland A's games before retiring. He was the 1979 recipient of the Ford C. Frick Award, bestowed annually by the National Baseball Hall of Fame.

176

Play-by-play man Bert Wilson was a diehard Cubs fan and made sure his radio listeners knew it. One of his famous lines was, "I don't care who wins, as long as it's the Cubs." He always made sure to mention "beautiful Wrigley Field."

A classic homer who practically invented the genre, Wilson loved all things Cubs during his time in the booth from 1944 to 1955. Trying to play off the Tinker-to-Evers-to-Chance double-play combination of an earlier Cubs era, he coined the phrase "Bingo to Bango to Bilko" when describing the combo of shortstop Ernie Banks, second baseman Gene Baker, and first baseman Steve Bilko.

Wilson got his big break with the Cubs when Bob Elson left the broadcast booth for World War II. During Elson's four-year absence, Wilson created such a loyal following for being such a loyal Cubs fan that the job was his to keep even after Elson's return. Once stateside, Elson switched over to White Sox broadcasts.

Though he got the chance to describe the Cubs' World Series run in 1945, much of Wilson's tenure was spent broadcasting Cubs losses.

BERT
WILSON

JACK QUINLAN

178

Jack Quinlan grew up a Cubs fan in Peoria, Illinois, and spent his entire broadcasting career—a much-too-short span from 1955 to '64—working for the Cubs during their golden era of broadcasting.

Beginning in 1958, Quinlan did play-by-play on WGN Radio and Lou Boudreau handled the color commentary.

One of the highlights of Quinlan's Cubs career was broadcasting Don Cardwell's no-hitter against the St. Louis Cardinals during a May 15, 1960, doubleheader at Wrigley Field. Cardwell was making his Cubs debut, two days after being acquired from the Philadelphia Phillies. It was the first no-hitter ever thrown by a pitcher in his first start with a new team.

That same season, Quinlan drew the plum assignment of broadcasting the World Series—between the Pittsburgh Pirates and New York Yankees—for NBC Radio. It turned out to be a classic World Series, with the Pirates' Bill Mazeroski winning Game 7 with a dramatic ninth-inning home run—becoming the first batter to end a World Series with a home run.

Quinlan's promising career was cut short during spring training in 1965, when he was killed in an automobile accident near the Cubs' spring training home in Arizona. He was 38.

VINCE LOU
LLOYD BOUDREAU

After play-by-play man Jack Quinlan's death in an automobile accident in 1965, Vince Lloyd was persuaded by Lou Boudreau to become his new partner in the booth.

That first season teaming with Boudreau, Lloyd enjoyed the highlight moment of his career, broadcasting left-hander Sandy Koufax's perfect game against the Cubs on September 9, 1965, called the greatest game ever pitched by the Society for American Baseball Research.

Lloyd became known as "The Voice of Summer," and aside from his trademark "Holy mackerel" call, he took to banging on a cow bell each time a Cub hit a home run during the 1970s.

After a Hall of Fame playing career that ended in 1952, and a managerial career that wrapped up in 1957, Boudreau returned home and took a job as a Cubs broadcaster.

But a month into the 1960 season, owner P. K. Wrigley summoned him from the broadcast booth and had him trade places with manager Charlie Grimm. The next season, Grimm retired and Boudreau returned to the booth.

Nicknamed "Good Kid," Boudreau could blend his knowledge as a player and manager and convey the nuances of the game to fans. He partnered in the Cubs radio booth for 20 years with Vince Lloyd, forming a golden-era broadcast team.

179

JACK BRICKHOUSE

Back, back, back . . . Hey-hey!"

When an 18-year-old Jack Brickhouse began working for his hometown radio station of WMBD in Peoria in 1934, he was the youngest announcer in the nation. Six years later, with some help from WGN pioneer Bob Elson, Brickhouse came to WGN, where he was to spend the next 41 years.

His trademark exclamation—"Hey-hey"—became such a big part of the Cubs experience, the team installed red "Hey-hey" signs along the towering foul poles down each line before the 1999 season.

WGN literally grew up with Brickhouse. When the station showed Chicago's first televised baseball game—an April 16, 1948, exhibition between the Cubs and White Sox at Wrigley Field—Brickhouse's face was the first image seen by viewers.

If you were a Chicago sports fan during the 1950s, '60s, or '70s, you heard Brickhouse describe the action. He worked for the Cubs, White Sox, Bulls, and Bears—but also interviewed popes and politicians. But he and the Cubs were intertwined, and Brickhouse broadcast more than 5,000 of their games. His style was more cheerleader than critic, and that endeared him to Chicago fans.

Brickhouse died in August 1998, six months after former WGN partner Harry Caray died.

The first statue erected outside Wrigley Field didn't honor a former Cubs player or manager, but a broadcaster. After his death in 1998, the team commissioned a statue to celebrate Harry Christopher Carabina—Harry Caray—who had become as synonymous with the Cubs as the bricks and ivy.

And the statue—on the corner of Addison and Sheffield streets—shows Caray in his most famous form, leading the seventh-inning stretch. In a practice that first became popular during his announcing days with the White Sox, Caray became a WGN icon leading Cubs fans at Wrigley Field in a loud round of "Take Me Out To The Ballgame," starting in classic style: "All right, let me hear ya. Ahhh-one. Ahhh-two. Ahhh-three. Take me out to the ballgame . . ." Caray used to say he liked the song because it was the only one he knew all the words to.

While early WGN partner Jack Brickhouse had his trademark "Hey-hey," Caray brought along his famous "Holy cow" line. Caray is said to have trained himself to exclaim "Holy cow" to avoid using profanity on the air. No matter the origin, the phrase became part of Cubs history.

Caray worked for the St. Louis Cardinals, White Sox, and one forgettable season with the Oakland Athletics before coming to the Cubs in 1981. Wrigley Field hasn't been the same since he arrived.

HARRY
CARAY

During his one season on the San Jose State basketball team as a rarely used reserve, Pat Hughes found a fun way to pass time. He would sit on the bench and do play-by-play for his teammates, and a career was born.

After 12 years working with Bob Uecker in the Milwaukee Brewers' broadcast booth, Hughes came to the Cubs in 1996 and offered the perfect balance with color commentator Ron Santo—blending a smooth delivery with Santo's passionate chatter.

One of the highlights of Hughes's career came in 1998, during the historic home-run chase between the Cubs' Sammy Sosa and the St. Louis Cardinals' Mark McGwire. When McGwire hit his 62nd home run—breaking Roger Maris's single-season record, Hughes said: "He drives one to deep left— this could be . . . it's a home run! Number 62 for Mark McGwire. A slice of history and a magical moment in St. Louis."

Cubs fans are more used to Hughes's smooth home-run call: "This ball's got a chaaance—gone!"

PAT   RON
HUGHES SANTO

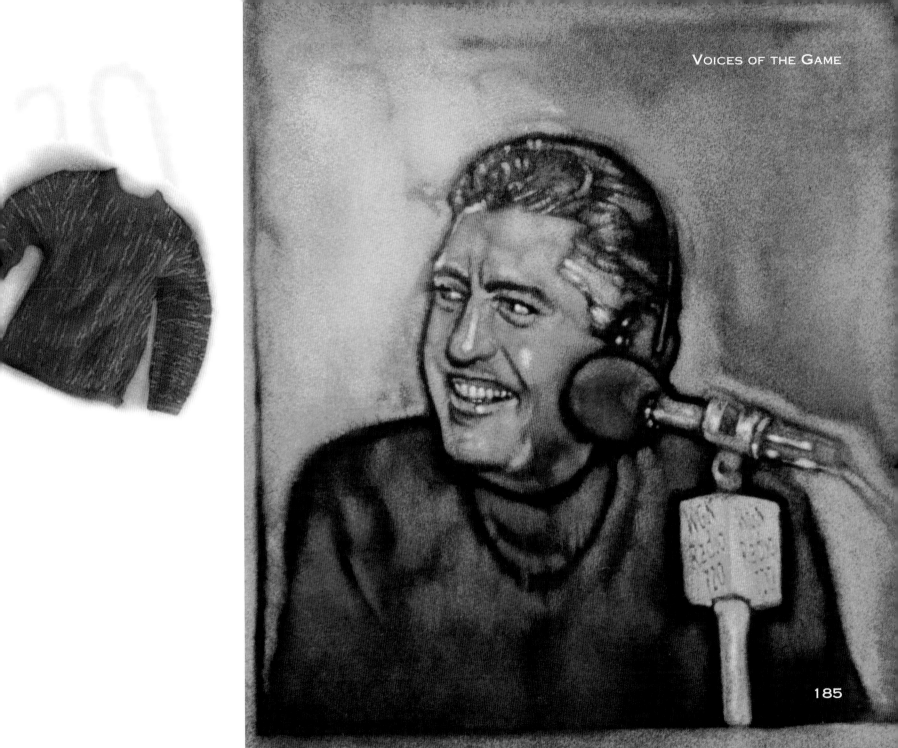

STEVE STONE

Right-hander Steve Stone, who pitched for the Cubs and White Sox during a playing career that peaked with 25 victories during a Cy Young season for the Baltimore Orioles in 1980, began his broadcasting career in 1982, after elbow trouble ended his pitching days.

ABC-TV quickly signed the insightful Stone and added him to its *Monday Night Baseball* team as a color analyst, sharing the booth with Al Michaels, Don Drysdale, and Howard Cosell. Right away, Stone showed a knack for breaking down the game and providing the kind of insight fans appreciated.

In 1983, he joined Harry Caray in the WGN-TV booth to form a successful tandem that lasted until Caray's death in 1998. "I think we had one of the best broadcast teams in baseball and in the history of the Cubs," Stone says. "Half our audience thought we were homers, the other half thought we were too critical, which tells you we did it right."

When Harry Caray died before the 1998 season, WGN hired his grandson Chip to join Stone in the booth. After a bumpy start—and a two-year break from 2000 to '02—Stone and Chip Caray became a solid team. Their tenure ended on a sour note, after the players and manager Dusty Baker turned on them, and Stone decided to walk away—disappointing fans more than the Cubs did that 2004 season.

INDEX

INDEX